50
Fun-Filled Sundays

Keep kids keen with a great
collection of games and activities
to complement your teaching

kevin mayhew

First published in 2006 by

KEVIN MAYHEW LTD
Buxhall, Stowmarket, Suffolk, IP14 3BW
info@kevinmayhewltd.com
www.kevinmayhew.com

50 Fun-filled Sundays is a compilation of various elements of the Powersource
Sunday school material first published by Kevin Mayhew in 2003. Various authors'
work has been included.

9 8 7 6 5 4 3 2 1 0

ISBN 1 84417 479 4
Catalogue No. 1500843

Edited and typeset by Graham Harris
Cover design by Angela Selfe

Printed and bound in Great Britain

CONTENTS

INTRODUCTION

50 Fun-filled Sundays is aimed at Sunday school leaders and children who want to enjoy themselves during their sessions together, as well as develop their relationships with each other and with God.

There are 'thinking' and 'doing' games, as well as opportunities to nurture acting talent and miming abilities. Prayer times are also suggested, and a 'talky bit' is provided to be used either straight from the page or as a springboard for your own ideas.

The sessions are mainly aimed at the younger primary school age group, but rather than sticking rigidly to what's available, use it as an inspiration to help you develop and adapt it to your own group's needs.

You might find that many of the activities and games prove so popular that your children will want to do them again, so don't limit their use to just what's suggested here.

The emphasis is not only on sharing the gospel message, but also on building trust with your children so that a true pastoral situation exists, enabling you as leader to minister to their needs and help their growth as Christians.

ACTIVITY 1

Footprints poster (or, more ambitiously, a banner)

Let the little children come to me and do not hinder them.
Mark 10:14

You will need
- A large sheet or banner-type material, with neatly hemmed edges and means of hanging once the work is complete
- Catalogues with pictures of small children and babies in them
- Glue
- Poster paint and brushes
- Large, flat trays in which to spread the paint
- Some bowls of warm, soapy water and towels
- A good team of helpers, appropriate to the size of your group

How it works
Help the children to cut out suitable pictures of children (and have some already cut out). Have the verse written out in large letters either on paper or, if you are making the banner, on material.

Have the large, flat trays with paint in them, with a helper or two beside each one, and with the bowls of water nearby.

Put the banner on the floor, take the children's shoes off, and get them to walk through the paint along the banner, from both ends. Have a yellow glow/smiley face in the middle that the little footprints are leading to. Display the banner in church when it is dry! (Make sure you wash and dry their feet thoroughly afterwards.)

Talky bit
Once everyone is dry and able to sit down in a group again, ask them to imagine a story about a famous footballer or a pop star visiting their school.

Tell the group about the excitement and anticipation.

The time of the visit arrived and the children were taken to the school hall to welcome the visitor. A large car arrived, with blacked out windows so nobody could see inside. A group of large men jumped out of the car and ran round to open the door for the star. The children cheered and they strained to see. A hand waved above the crowd of people.

A small boy stepped forward to greet his hero on behalf of the whole school. The men surrounding the star closed up so that the boy could not get through.

A huge wave of disappointment swept through the children. Suddenly, the star's voice could be heard. 'Don't stand in the way. I've come to see the children. They are my friends.'

It's likely that one of your group will mention that this reminds them of a story in the Bible; use this springboard to relate the whole story from Mark 10:14.

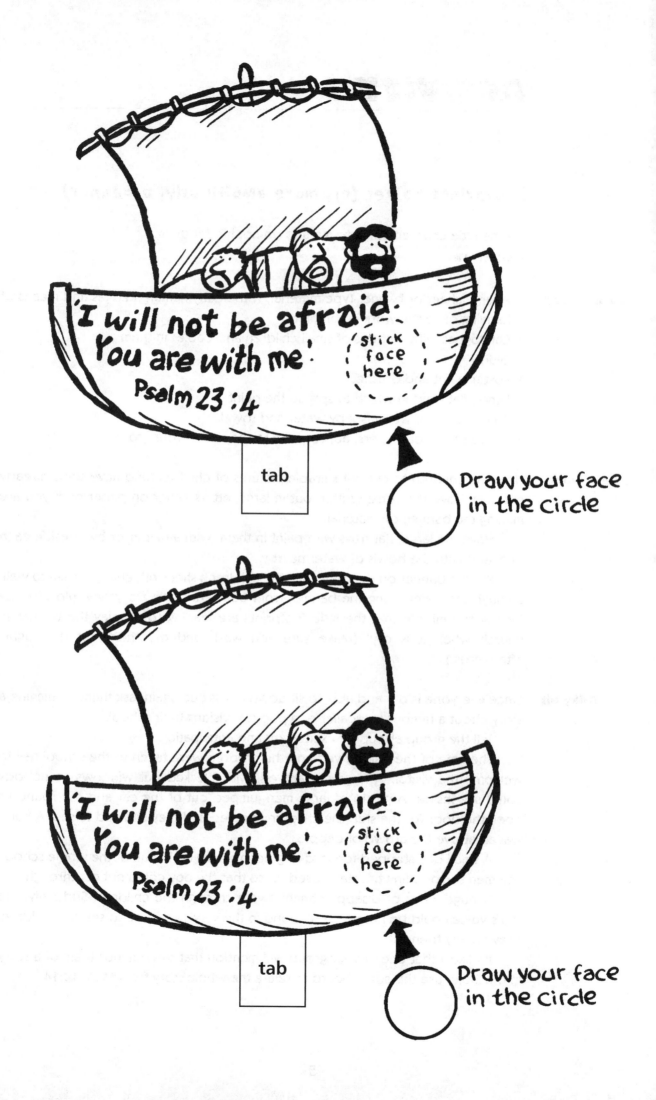

ACTIVITY 2

Noah's Ark experiment!

I will not be afraid. You are with me.
Psalm 23:4

You will need
- A variety of small containers (polystyrene trays, margarine tubs, etc.), some of which might not float
- Some small toy animals to go in the 'boats'
- Some bowls or buckets in which to launch them
- Towels for drying hands or mopping up
- Photocopy the boat shapes (page 6) and glue on to card
- Paper circles for drawings of children's faces

How it works
Children can experiment with making boats for small toy animals. Show them the variety of containers available. Ask them which they think will float (explain as necessary). Test them all, keeping those that float together. Ask them to find one of these that will float with an animal in. What about a boat that could stay afloat with hundreds of animals in it? God knew just what sort of boat would, and told Noah all about it in detail.

Talky bit
Explain that today's verse was something King David wrote many years after the actual event took place. When he was a shepherd boy, he learnt that even when he was very lonely, looking after his sheep, God was always there.

Hand out the cut-out boat shapes and small pieces of paper. Ask children to draw a picture of their face and stick it by the word 'me'.

Discuss what this means to us every day, identifying places/situations in which Jesus will be with the children.

ACTIVITY 3

Jonah and the big fish

Jesus said: 'I am with you always.'
Matthew 28:20

You will need
- An area of the room set up to represent a boat, e.g. a blanket large enough for all the children to get onto or some small benches or chairs arranged to look like a rowing boat
- A tape/CD player with suitable tape or CD
- A box to contain your props for the story (props are: toy boat, coin, ticket, large white/blue fabric to simulate wave (see story), some small boxes and a large paper fish

How it works This game can be played in either of the ways shown below, dependent on time.

Game 1

1. Explain to the children about the boat, and that the floor is the sea.
2. Get them to sit together in the boat. When the music starts they must row the boat in the way you tell them to, e.g. slowly, gently, quickly, strongly.
3. When the music stops they all fall out of the boat and splash into the sea.
4. Repeat as many times as you want to!

Game 2

1. Explain to the children about the boat, and that the floor is the sea.
2. Get them to find a space in the sea. When the music starts, they must swim around in the sea in the way you tell them to, e.g. slowly, quickly, forward, backward.
3. When the music stops they jump up out of the sea and find a place in the boat.
4. Repeat as many times as you want to!

At the end of the game, settle everyone down and explain that they will soon be finding out more about boats and the sea. Continue by using the story of Jonah and the big fish. This story is interactive, so encourage the children to mirror your actions.

Talky bit
Narrator 1 Good morning, seafarers, it's good to see that you're all safe and sound and back on dry land after that adventure. In the Bible Jesus said: 'I am with you always' (Matthew 28:20). 'My strength (flex arm muscles) comes from God (point upwards) who never (shake pointing finger and head) dozes or sleeps' (head on folded hands, eyes closed) Psalm 121.

Repeat the verse and actions two or three times and then sit down. Quieten the children, ready to listen.

Let's see what we have in here. (*Take out the toy boat*) It's a boat! I know a song about a boat; sing it with me. (*Pretend to row the boat as you sing.*)

Row, row, row your boat, gently down the stream,
if you see a crocodile, don't forget to scream! (Children scream)

Here's another way to sing that song; join in with me:

Row, row, row your boat, over the deep blue sea,
if you see a great big fish, don't forget to scream! (Children scream)
(*Repeat a couple of times.*)

Settle the children down to watch and listen.

Narrator 1 Our story from the Bible begins with a man called Jonah. God told Jonah to go from where he lived to a big city called Nineveh, and tell the people who lived there that God was not happy with them because they were bad.
But Jonah wasn't happy with what God wanted him to do.

Narrator 2 What did you say, God? You want me to go and tell those people that you're not happy with them? Who? Me? Me? (*Points at self*) . . . You must be joking!

Narrator 1 But God was not joking.

Narrator 2 What's that you're saying God? . . . You're not joking!
Well God, I'm not joking either. I am not going to Nineveh – never, never, never.

Narrator 1 So Jonah ran and ran until he found a . . . (*Show the toy boat and get the children to guess what it was that Jonah found.*) BOAT. It was getting ready to go out to sea.
Now what do we have next in our box? (*Take out a coin and a ticket and give it to Narrator 2, who does the actions to the story.*) Jonah gave the captain of the boat some money for a ticket, got on the boat, and it started to sail out to sea.
Let's pretend we're in the boat with Jonah and row the boat out to sea. (*Pretend to row, singing the rowing song several times.*)
As they rowed, Jonah chatted to the other sailors, and they laughed and sang until – all of a sudden – what happened? Open the box to find out what came next. (*Take a large piece of white/blue fabric from the box.*)

Narrator 1 God sent a great big wind over the sea. All blow hard and make loud wind sounds!
Let's see what happens to the sea when there's a great big wind!
(*Adults and children stand and hold each end, both sides of the fabric; as they blow, they make the fabric go up and down like huge waves.*)

Narrator 1 The waves kept getting higher. (*Continue to make the fabric go up and down.*)
The thunder crashed. (*Get the children to stamp their feet for thunder.*)
And the boat began to rock about on the sea. Hey, everyone, stop the waves for a moment. Stay where you are. We need the next thing from our box.
(*Take out some smaller boxes and give one each to some of the children.*)

Narrator 1 The boat was carrying lots of heavy boxes and so the sailors decided to get rid of them and throw them into the sea. If you have a box, throw it into the sea (*fabric*), then everyone come and sit down for the rest of the story.
(*Narrator 2 joins the circle, but curls up as if sleeping.*)

Narrator 1 What was Jonah doing during the storm? (*Point to Narrator 2, who pretends to sleep.*)

9

He was sleeping! Let's call to Jonah to wake up: 'Wake up Jonah, wake up!' (*Jonah wakes up.*)

'Come on, Jonah, get up,' said the sailors. 'We need you to pray and ask your God to save us from this storm.'

Narrator 2   Oh I'm sorry, I'm really sorry. I haven't done what God asked me to do and I have run away to sea to get away from him. But God is with us wherever we are and we can never get away from him. This storm is all my fault. Pick me up and throw me into the sea and then you will be saved.

Narrator 1   And so the sailors got hold of Jonah, called out to God to save them, and threw Jonah into the sea!

As Jonah disappeared into the stormy sea, the big waves stopped! The sailors said thank you to God for saving them.

But what has happened to Jonah? Where is he? Has God saved Jonah too?

Let's see what's left in the box.

(*Take out the great big fish. Roll it out onto the floor away from the children and Narrator 2 goes and lies down on it.*)

Narrator 1   Come on, let's sing:

Row, row, row your boat, over the deep blue sea,
if you see a great big fish, don't forget to scream!

Narrator 2   Oh, God, I'm so sorry for running away. I'm so sorry for not doing as you said. I'm sorry I was disobedient. Please forgive me. Thank you God that you are always with me. Thank you that my strength comes from you. You never doze or sleep.

Narrator 1   God had sent a great big fish to swallow up Jonah and keep him safe from the storm. Jonah prayed from inside the belly of the fish.

Then God made the great big fish cough up Jonah from out of his belly. Jonah was safe. The sailors were safe.

And do you know what Jonah did next? He went all the way to Nineveh, just as God had told him to, and he spoke to the people there to tell them that God was not happy with them and that they were to stop doing bad things. And they stopped their bad ways and God was pleased with them. God was with Jonah on the boat, in the belly of the great big fish, and in Nineveh. And God is always with us, too.

Remember what Jesus said? Jesus said: 'I am with you always' (Matthew 28:20).
(*Encourage everyone to say and do as you do.*)
'My strength (*flex muscles*) comes from God (*point upwards*) who never dozes or sleeps' (*head on hands, eyes closed*) Psalm 121.

ACTIVITY 4

Group prayer scrapbook

Call to me and I will answer you.
Jeremiah 33:3

You will need
- A large scrapbook
- Gummed stars, shapes, glitter glue, crayons, felt pens – anything that you know your children love using to decorate and write with
- Sheets of paper, varying colours if you like, but white will do
- Safety scissors

How it works This activity can be used as an extension activity when the service looks like lasting a little longer than you anticipated, or if Communion means that your session will be longer than normal.

Talky bit How often do you use the phone? Have you learned how to dial yet? (Even very young ones should have been told about the emergency numbers.) See if they can tell you (don't be surprised if 911 crops up, because so many children are influenced by US television). If your group is slightly older you could see if any of them know any phone numbers yet. You could reel off a couple of those that you know off by heart, and you can mention that a person on one of the numbers (a close friend or relative) will always respond quickly if you ask them for help.

Sometimes, though, there's a problem (you could mimmick the engaged tone and see if anyone recognises it). Explain that sometimes you can't get through to the person you want to speak to and a voice might say: 'The person you wish to speak to is on the phone at the moment – please leave a message.'

It might be that they are speaking to someone else; but in the Bible God tells his people: 'Call to me and I will answer you' (Jeremiah 33:3).

So, there you have it – God's phone number is 333. That's easy to remember – 'Call to me and I will answer you.'

At this point it's important to stress that the children shouldn't actually pick up the phone and dial 333, but that you're using the verse from Jeremiah 33:3 to illustrate the point.

To finish
Focus on God's care. Begin a prayer scrapbook – to be continued whenever the opportunity arises. Talk about different types of prayer – thanks, pleas, praise, prayers for others – labelling (with words/symbols/pictures) a page for each.

Encourage the children to draw carefully or write a couple of words for one of those types of prayer, explaining that when they've finished they will stick their 'prayer' in the scrapbook, to be built up over the weeks ahead. Remind the children that they are 'calling to God' through their prayers, and he has promised to answer their call.

ACTIVITY 5

Feelings – plates

I will not be afraid. You are with me.
Psalm 23:4

You will need Paper plates – enough for your group to have two each, plus some spares for guests.

How it works On the paper plates (two per child), draw eyes/noses; discuss how our mouths look when we're happy/sad. Show the chilrdren how to make happy and sad faces on the plates. Explain that we are going to use the plates to help us pray today. Use the sad plates while you spend time together thinking about anything you have done for which you want to say sorry.

Draw these things together into a leader's prayer at the end, or invite the children to pray. Then hold up the happy plates, while you thank Jesus for listening and for forgiving you.

The prayer plates can be coloured, ready to use at other times. Discuss with the children how they could draw a 'frightened' plate to use in this story. For instance, some could stick cut-out hands over the eyes of their plates.

Talky bit God knows how we feel. He knows that we sometimes feel really upset, and that we might not feel like talking to anybody. He also knows that sometimes we get so excited that we talk quickly and without thinking, so that we might not make any sense to mum or dad or whoever we're with. They sometimes say: 'Slow down and start again, this time more slowly.' Have you ever had anyone say that to you?

God wants to hear us speak to him at any time, however we're feeling, and the words we use and the way we say them will be just right. He knows what we're feeling and what we really want to say to him.

ACTIVITY 6

Nurturing growth

God is our help.
Isaiah 41:13

You will need
- Empty yoghurt pot and cotton wool for each child. Either cover each pot with white paper, or stick on a face shape
- Mustard and cress seeds
- Coloured adhesive shapes for decoration
- Water

How it works
Decorate your own seed pot and plant some seeds. Give each child an empty yoghurt pot either covered with: a) white paper; or b) a paper face shape stuck onto it.

For a) allow the children to draw patterns on the pot to make a colourful vase; or for b) allow them to draw a face on the paper shape (no hair as the seedlings will take that role!).

Put damp cotton wool into each pot and sprinkle a few seeds on top (children can do this with a little supervision). They take the pot home at the end of the session with instructions to water it a little every day and keep it where the sun will shine on it.

Talky bit
Learn the verse of Scripture. Try repeating it with the children. Then add a simple clap to each word. Vary that with a tap on the knee for each word. Then get really adventurous by putting a pattern of claps and taps together, i.e. clap each word, then tap knees on each word and finally clap hands for first word, knees for the second word, hands for the third word and knees for the last word.

Tell the children that just as they will be keen to see how their seeds grow, and just as they will be eagerly checking progress and adding just the right amount of water each day to ensure growth, God is watching over them with just as much interest to see how they grow and develop.

And God knows just what we need to help us do that. Not too much, and not too little, but just the right things that we need.

ACTIVITY 7

God knows us very well

Lord . . . you are familiar with all my ways.
Psalm 139:3

You will need
- A large mirror
- Circles of card
- Circles of silver foil to cover the card
- Glue sticks
- Alternatively, use adhesive mirror foil, available from craft shops (it has a better reflection, though it is more expensive)
- Scraps of hair-coloured wool
- Pictures of faces taken from a magazine, newspaper or catalogue

How it works
Remind the children that people are part of God's creation. Show the children the pictures of faces and allow them to talk about the differences. You may like to tell them that a blind person may want to feel a face to 'see' what it is like. (You could try this, by blindfolding a helper – unless a child is willing to be blindfolded – and seeing if they recognise a child by gently running their fingers over the child's face.)

All these faces are very different and when you look at all the children you can see how different they are. Show a mirror and let the children look at themselves. Then show one of the safe mirrors you have made and tell the children they will be making similar mirrors to take home and remind themselves how much God loves them and has made them all different.

Let the children make up the 'mirrors', adding scraps of wool round the top edge for 'hair'.

Write the child's name on their mirror.

Talky bit
Sometimes we ask people at school 'Who's your best friend?' In one way it's a shame that people should expect us to choose, because it's good to have lots of friends. But it is nice to have special friends, with whom we build up a very strong relationship. Maybe mum or dad or the person who looks after you has a special friend they've known for a long, long time.

The thing about really special friends is that they stay with you – even if something horrible happens.

Think about Jesus as your very special friend. He knows all about you and cares about you. He'll always be ready to hear and help whenever you need it.

ACTIVITY 8

Fingerprint painting

God saw all that he had made, and it was very good.
Genesis 1:31

You will need
- A fingerprint, suitably enlarged via a photocopier, to show the pattern
- Smaller fingerprints
- A sample fingerprint picture (unless you want to do one quickly at the time)
- Finger paints in a variety of colours
- Shallow containers for paints
- Paper in different shapes and sizes (A4, A5, circles, triangles, etc.)
- Aprons or old shirts to protect clothing
- Hand-washing facilities
- Crayons to add decoration and name art work

How it works
Explain to the children that everyone has something that is theirs only. Nobody else can have one like it.

Show the fingerprint and explain that no one else has one just the same. Show them the other fingerprints you have made. Explain that the group is going to make fingerprint pictures to help remember that we are all special – unique – and that God loves us very much.

Show a fingerprint picture already created (uttering the time-honoured phrase: 'Here's one I made earlier'), or make one very quickly and simply in front of the children. (If you are working with very young children use handprints instead.)

Remind the children to use different fingertips for different colours of paint.

Talky bit
God loves us all so much and he knows just how wonderfully we are made because he made us. He wants us to be caring towards the rest of his creation, all the plants and animals and other people, but we need God's help to do this and to be kind and loving.

Use this as a springboard into prayer to thank God for his creation and to ask for his help to look after it.

ACTIVITY 9

Smiley-face fridge magnet

'Do not fear; I will help you,' says the Lord.
Isaiah 41:13

You will need
- 5cm diameter circles of white/pale card
- Felt pens/crayons
- Scraps of wool for hair
- Glue
- Safe scissors
- Magnetic strip (available from craft shops)
- Sticky tape
- A completed 'smiley face' to show the children
- Lunch box for the story (Talky bit)

How it works
Decorate a circle of card to look like a smiley face. This has a magnetic strip on the back so that they can stick it to the fridge/washing machine, etc. and it will cheer up their parent/special adult whenever they see it. Show one of the finished smiley-face fridge magnets and then assist the children with making theirs.

Talky bit
Relate the story of the feeding of the 5000 (John 6:1-15). Familiarise yourself with the story and talk about it with a simple puppet (a hand inside a clean sock will be fine). Nod and shake the puppet's head at the appropriate moment. Try to use your own words and bring the story to life, but here's a suggested script.

One day Jesus was talking to a lot of people – more people than are here in this room (*puppet opens mouth in amazement*); more people than are here in this building (*puppet opens mouth wider*); more people than the pupils in your school (*very wide-mouthed puppet*). In fact, so many people that they would fill one end of a stadium. (*Puppet 'faints' in asonishment.*)

It was getting late and everyone's tummy was rumbling. (*Encourage children to rub tummies, while you rub the puppet's.*)

Then Jesus asked one of his special friends, called Philip: 'Where can we buy enough bread for all these people to eat?' But Philip didn't know. (*Children and puppet shake heads.*)

Then another one of Jesus' friends came up and said: 'Here is a little boy with some bread and fish – but not enough for all these people.' (*Open the lunch box and let the children look inside. Stress how that wouldn't be enough for just a few people and definitely not enough for the big crowd with Jesus.*)

But then Jesus said thank you to God and told all the people to sit down and his friends would share it out.

And there was enough to go around. In fact there was more than enough to go around. There were baskets full of food left over. (*Puppet is happy.*)

I expect that little boy felt very important – to Jesus everyone is important whether you are big or small and whatever you give to Jesus he can use. (*Puppet looks sad.*)

The puppet is still a bit sad because he can't think of anything that he could do to help. You explain that the puppet has been a great help because he's helped you tell the story, and then take this idea further in encouraging the children to help you cheer the puppet up, by smiling.

This works and go on to try this 'skill' out on others around. See if there are any 'sad looking' adults in the room (prompt an adult to look sad before telling the story). Let the children try out their smiles on that adult. It will work (of course – who can resist a child's smile?). And then go on to say that God loves us and wants us to be happy, and just like they made the puppet and the adult happy again the children can make others around them happy. Close with a simple prayer to ask God to help us share his love with others.

ACTIVITY 10

Sharing and giving

And do not forget to do good and to share with others.
Hebrews 13:16

You will need
- Two plain biscuits per child (plus some for breakages)
- Decorative icing
- Decorations
- Plastic bags to take biscuits home in

or

- Circles of card for pretend biscuits
- Felt pens or crayons
- Glue
- Decorations (sequins, tissue paper, etc.)
- Safety scissors

How it works

Idea 1: (10 mins – longer if time allows)
Decorate two biscuits – very simply (rather messy). One biscuit is to be taken home, and the other biscuit is to be given to another child in the session (all will receive a biscuit but not the one they decorated). When biscuits are decorated sit all the children down and let them choose to give their biscuit to another child.

Make sure that each child receives a biscuit by encouraging each child to choose someone who hasn't had a biscuit yet. Enjoy them! Take remaining biscuit home.

Idea 2: (10 mins – but have ready-cut shapes and a glue stick!)
Decorate a pretend biscuit. Using glue, sequins, felt pens, etc., let the children decorate a biscuit-shaped piece of card to give away. Decorate another biscuit-shaped card to take home.

Write the verse in the centre of each 'biscuit'. When all the 'biscuits' are decorated sit all the children down and let them choose to give their 'biscuit' to another child at the session. Enjoy how beautifully decorated they are. Take the remaining 'biscuit' home to share.

Talky bit
God is pleased when we share what we have with others. Everything that we have comes from God, so it makes him very happy to see us sharing his gifts to us with our friends and familly.

ACTIVITY 11

'Seeing' with your hands, giving praise for God's goodness

I will give thanks and praise to God.
Daniel 2:23

You will need
- Paper and felt pens or crayons to make a picture of the story
- A number of different objects in a bag
- Make a recording of different everyday sounds – e.g. telephone ringing, tap dripping, toilet flushing, etc., or see if the library has a sound-effects CD
- Draw a picture of the story of Bartimaeus (from Mark 10:46-52) or invite someone who is a good artist in your church to produce a few key illustrations. This is a good way of involving other people in your Sunday school work.

How it works
Put a number of different objects in a bag. Ask the children to close their eyes, put their hand in the bag and guess what one of the objects is. For young children it may be appropriate to show them the objects first before putting them into the bag.

Play the sounds you have recorded, one by one, and ask the children to listen and to guess what the sound is. To prevent one alert child guessing them all, put the children in groups of threes and allocate each sound to a group. This is an inclusive way of sharing the activity.

Talky bit
Explain the relevance of the above activities to the story of Bartimaeus. Explain that before Bartimaeus was healed he would have had to listen very carefully to know where he was and what was around him.

He would have used his touch to identify everyday objects, he would have recognised his friends by the sound of their voices or maybe the sound they made as they approached him.

Use the illustrations to tell the story of Bartimaeus in your own words, with the following outline to help you.

Jesus was leaving Jericho with his disciples and a lot of people were following him. A man called Bartimaeus was sitting at the side of the road as Jesus went past. He was blind. Can you see Bartimaeus? Bartimaeus knew that Jesus was not very far away so he shouted: 'Jesus help me.'

The people who were beside Bartimaeus said: 'Be quiet.'

But Bartimaeus shouted again: 'Jesus help me.' Jesus heard Bartimaeus and asked him to come to him.

Bartimaeus tore off his old coat, threw it to the ground, jumped up and went to Jesus.

Jesus said: 'What do you want me to do?' Bartimaeus said: 'I want to see.'

Jesus said: 'You can see. You believed that I could heal you so it has happened. Your faith has healed you.'

Bartimaeus was amazed – he could see. As Jesus went off down the road Bartimaeus followed him.

Conclude by asking if the children noticed anything important about the last sentence of the story.

Remind them that you said: 'As Jesus went off down the road Bartimaeus followed him.'

Bartimaeus was so thankful at what Jesus had done that he wanted to follow him. Draw out the fact that many people are so grateful about what Jesus has done that they follow him today. They follow his teaching from the Bible, they talk to him daily as their friend, and they read all about him in the Bible so that they might get to know more and more about him.

ACTIVITY 12

Get-well card

When Jesus saw their faith, he said to the paralytic, 'Son, your sins are forgiven.'
Mark 2:5 (NIV)

You will need
- Paper and felt pens or crayons for drawing a picture of the story
- An A4 sheet of paper or card folded in half for each child
- Simple illustration to accompany your telling of the story, either drawn by you or someone you know who is good at drawing (give them plenty of notice)

How it works
Invite the children to make a 'get well' card for someone they know is not well. Give each child an A4 sheet of paper or card folded in half. Put a small mark on the front page to show the children which page to draw their picture. After the children have drawn their pictures ask them to tell you what they would like to have written inside.

Talky bit
Tell the story in your own words, using the Bible as your base (Mark 2:1-12), or by fleshing out the script below, bringing it to life as much as you can.

> One day, Jesus was teaching at a house in a village. Some men walked towards the house carrying a man on a sleeping mat. The man could not walk. The men tried to push through the crowd to Jesus but they could not reach him.
>
> They decided to go up on to the flat roof. They climbed up the steps, took off some of the tiles to make a hole in the roof and gently lowered their friend down into the house, right in front of Jesus.
>
> Jesus saw the man on the sleeping mat and said: 'Your sins are forgiven.' (Explain to the children that Jesus knew the wrong things that the man had done and he would forget all of them.) Some of the people who heard this did not like what Jesus had said.
>
> Jesus said to the man: 'Get up, roll up your sleeping mat and go home.'
>
> Immediately the man jumped to his feet, picked up his mat and went home praising God. Everyone was really surprised at what they had seen.

Remind the children that if God feels it is the best thing for someone to be healed then he will heal them.

ACTIVITY 13

Animal masks. For a Christmas-time session

The baby was called Jesus.
Luke 2:21

You will need
- Paper plates (one for each child) to make animal masks. Cut eye holes in preparation
- Ear or horn shapes, tissue, wool, etc. to stick on as appropriate
- Paint and brushes (though this may take time to dry)
- Sticks and sticky tape if you wish to mount the masks this way
- Play dough (recipe is on page 23)
- Nativity-scene cutters or relevant animal cutters from craft shop
- A Christmas stocking or Christmas tree drawing for the children to attach their 'presents' to after prayer time at the end of the session: some blank labels for that, plus a simple drawing of a present

How it works
Use paper plates and collage with tissue paper, adding ears, horns, etc., to make the animal look realistic. Leader either attaches elastic or a stick to hold mask in front of face.

Use Nativity-scene cutters or animal cutters to make the animals from the play dough. Otherwise the children may simply try to model an animal of their choice.

Talky bit
Nativity scene
Let the children act out the Nativity scene as you tell the story. If you don't want to risk spoiling the models made by the children you could use the following method.

Have ready a manger with baby Jesus lying in it.

Have bags with Nativity scene pieces in. Number the bags and have the following pieces in them:
1. Mary and Joseph
2. Animals
3. Shepherds and sheep
4. Angels

Show the children the manger and the baby first.

Ask a child to put their hand in the bag (in numerical order) and pick an object. Can the child guess what it is by feeling it? Then the child takes the piece out and places it where they think it should be within the Nativity scene. Do they know who the character is? If it is an animal, would they like to live with that animal? Would it be noisy/quiet? What would it smell like? As each animal is mentioned make the appropriate noise and action.

Tell the Christmas story from Luke 2:1-20, perhaps using a children's Bible version. Gently press home the fact that although it is a time for getting presents, the main reason is to celebrate Jesus' birthday.

Close with a group prayer time. Introduce it by inviting the children to name the presents Jesus was given.

Remind them that although they probably enjoy receiving presents, as they grow older they might take just as much pleasure in giving presents.

The best present we can give Jesus is our love. He doesn't need or want a present – he just wants to be our friend. Ask the children if they want to be Jesus' friend and will love him. If they do, ask them to draw their face or write their name if they can on a label attached to a 'present' (the prepared drawing or picture, cut out). Tell the children to attach their 'present' with some Blu-Tack to the cut-out Christmas tree or Christmas stocking.

Pray a simple prayer that the children can say after you. For example: 'Jesus, my present to you for Christmas is that I will be your friend. Amen.'

Play-dough recipe

Ingredients
2 cups flour
2 cups water
1 cup salt
1 tablespoon oil
1 tablespoon cream of tartar
Food colouring

Method
Put all the ingredients in a saucepan and cook until it all sticks together.

JESUS
JUST WHAT WE NEED!
SHEPHERD
KING
REIGNING FOR EVER!
SAVIOUR
IMMANUEL

ACTIVITY 14

Parcel fun! Christmas – it's just what we need

God loved the world so much that he gave his only Son.
John 3:16

You will need
- Two identical selections of four to six parcels wrapped in Christmas paper at the front of the room
- A chair at the side to mark the other end of the course
- Four cards each with a part of the verse written in large letters – God loved the world so much that he gave his only Son. (John 3:16)

How it works *Piles of parcels relay*

If you feel your group is old enough, you could extend this game to include a little 'life skills' activity – learning to wrap a parcel.

If you decide to do this you will need to add some paper, sticky tape, ribbon, scissors (safety) to your 'You will need' list above. It is well worth including this activity if you're able. The children enjoy it and parents or carers will be delighted that they have learned how to wrap things up.

For the game itself . . .
The children need to be split into two large groups and from each of these you need to select a pair of children to play the game. The remainder of the children can cheer their team on.

One player in each team stands by the parcels at the front of the room, the other player has to have one hand behind his/her back and the other stretched out in front to hold the parcels. It is important that only one hand is ever used by player two.

Play begins when player one places the first parcel on player two's outstretched hand. Player two then has to walk as quickly as possible round the chair and back to the front, where player one balances the second parcel on top of the first and player two walks round the course again. Play continues in this manner with an ever-increasing pile of parcels.

The game is won by the first team to complete the course with all their parcels. A dropped parcel disqualifies that team and the other team wins by default.

If you have time you could split each team into several pairs and have several heats. The overall winners would then be the team with the most wins.

World poster
The group could produce a poster which sums up what you have been thinking about today; this might be displayed, perhaps on a wall in church, to form a focal

point for the church's intercessions over the Christmas season (see page 24 for an example, but your children should use this only to kick-start their ideas).

Talky bit   The game we played reminds us that sometimes there are so many presents at Christmas time that it's a bit of a balancing act to keep up with it all.

The posters the children design will be a great reminder to everyone who visits the church over Christmas, that Jesus is the Christmas gift who is 'just what we need'.

As part of your celebrations and anticipation of Christmas you could have fun by learning the verse (John 3:16) together as a Mexican wave.

Split the group into four smaller groups. Allocate each group one part of the verse.

Produce the four cards each with a part of the verse and have one child per group stand at the front and hold the card up for their group to read.

ACTIVITY 15

Christmas celebration party

The baby was called Jesus.
Luke 2:21

You will need
- Crown template (and some cut out already for less able children)
- 'Jesus is King' labels
- Coloured adhesive shapes, etc. for decorating the crowns
- Safety scissors

How it works

Crowns

Have crown shapes already prepared. If you have more able children they could cut their own out. Stick on gummed shapes, sequins, glitter and 'Jesus is King' label.

The Christmas story

Luke 2:1-20 and Matthew 2:1-12

Sit the children in a semi-circle so they can all see and so that there is an open area in which the children can act. As you tell the story, simply act it out with them as you go along, so the children are incorporated and doing something rather than sitting still.

The children may have to fulfil more than one role depending on the number of children in your group. Mary and Joseph need to be specifically allocated those roles because they are in the story throughout. You can have varying numbers of angels, shepherds and wise men to allow all children to be involved (make sure you have enough props/visual aids for them so no one is left out).

You may wish to indicate in the beginning which role each child will play and give them their visual aid/prop. If you do not have as many children and they are playing more than one role, you may want to give them their roles as they appear in the story.

Child 1 – Mary (with doll)
Child 2 – Joseph (tea towel for head-dress)
Child 3 – Innkeeper
Shepherds – (sheep/tea towels)
Wise men – (crowns)
Angels – (tinsel)

Mary and Joseph travelled to Bethlehem (*child 1 and child 2 walk from one side of semi-circle to other*).

When Mary and Joseph got to Bethlehem, they were very tired (*child 1 and 2 yawn*). So Mary and Joseph looked for somewhere to stay. Joseph knocked on lots of doors (*child 2 pretends to knock on doors*).

But all the inns were full (*children shake heads*).

Joseph then knocked on the last door (*child 2 pretends to knock on door*). The innkeeper said: 'Sorry, I have no room in the inn but you can stay in the stable' (*child 3 shakes his head and then points to a space; all three move to a part of the semi-circle; child 3 leaves them*).

That night Mary had a baby boy (*child 1 holds doll*).

Mary laid him in a manger and called him Jesus (*child 1 lies the doll down in front of them. Child 2 sits by the doll*).

(*Shepherds sit in the middle of the semi-circle.*)

Some angels (*angels stand in front of the shepherds*) came to some shepherds who were looking after their sheep.

They told the shepherds that a new king had been born (*angels point to where Mary, Joseph and the baby are*).

(*Angels sit back down in their places.*)

The shepherds went to visit baby Jesus. Perhaps they gave him a gift – a lamb, maybe? (*Shepherds walk to where Mary and Joseph are, one gives a lamb/sheep and they sit down with them.*)

Some time later, after the shepherds had left, Mary and Joseph moved to a little house (*shepherds sit back down in their places. Mary and Joseph walk to another area*).

When Jesus was a bit bigger some wise men (*wise men stand up*) came to worship Jesus and brought him gifts (*wise men walk to where Mary and Joseph are and sit with them*).

People gave gifts to Jesus when he was a baby, but in a special way Jesus was a gift to us from Father God.

You might like to sing a Christmas song.

Talky bit   Recap on the teaching by asking simple questions:

Who was born at Christmas? Jesus

Who came to visit Jesus when he was a bit bigger? Wise men

How do we remember when we were born? Birthdays (you may need some visual clues – hat, party invitation, balloons, cake, etc.).

How could we remember the day Jesus was born? Have a party

The best gift we could give to Jesus is ourselves – to be his friends, and for him to be our best friend. Let's say thank you to Jesus and have a little party!

(*Start the music and have a small party with some prepared food.*)
Invite the children to wear the crowns they made earlier.

Have a cake and sing 'Happy Birthday' to Jesus.

Play a couple of games, e.g. pass the parcel and hunt the stars (*the children search for the stars – they need to find two each, one for each hand*). If they have found two they could help someone else. Swap the stars for some Smarties or other appropriate small sweets.

Finish the party with a Christmas song.

ACTIVITY 16

Choices – pass the parcel

Remember the Lord in everything you do and he will show you the right way.
Proverbs 3:6 (Good News Bible)

You will need   Pass the parcel game, with Smarties and small stones (as described).

How it works   Wrap up two parcels for a game of pass the parcel. Each parcel needs to have the same number of wrappings (not too many, or the game could take a long time!).

One parcel needs to have very attractive wrappings throughout, while the other needs to be wrapped in newspaper or other scrappy looking paper. Place a Smarties tube full of stones in the parcel with the attractive wrappings and place a real tube of Smarties in the parcel with the newspaper wrapping. Keep the spare Smarties to share after the game.

If you have enough children divide them into two groups. Show the children the two parcels. Which would they prefer? Give each group a parcel. (You might have some reactions of 'unfair' from the group with the newspaper parcel.) Play a game of pass the parcel. Finally, when the parcel is opened up the groups will see which is the better. The groups who had the newspaper parcel can share their reward. After this you can 'give in' and hand out the spare Smarties to the other group!

Tell the children that the story today is about Abraham finding a wife for Isaac and so it was very important to make the right choice.

Talky bit   Many years had gone by since God had tested Abraham to see if he would sacrifice his only son. Isaac had grown up and it was time for him to get married. Sarah had died and Abraham knew it was very important to find just the right wife for Isaac. Abraham trusted God totally and believed that God had already chosen who that should be. So today we are going to hear how it all happened.

Tell, rather than read, the story from Genesis 24. Read the story yourself and use the following key points written on a card as a reminder, if you need them.

- Abraham sends his servant back to the land he came from. Explain why.
- Servant worried. What if she won't come? Take Isaac back to homeland?
- Servant sets out and reaches the well outside Nahor's city.
- Servant worried about knowing who to choose. Prays.
- Makes a plan with God as to how it might happen.
- Rebekah comes back to the well.
- Servant puts plan into operation.
- Rebekah fulfils the plan. She's related (her grandfather was Abraham's brother).
- Servant explains why he has come.
- Rebekah agrees to leave her home and go with the servant to Canaan to meet Isaac. Isaac meets Rebekah. It's love at first sight! All with God's help!

ACTIVITY 17

Decorative invitations

Everyone who calls on the name of the Lord will be saved.
Acts 2:21

You will need
- Large plant/fake tree
- Doll or puppet (to be Zacchaeus)
- Purse of money
- Invitations – one for each child – with the Memory verse on the back (Acts 2:21)
- Pens/crayons
- Glue
- Scissors
- Catalogue pages, with pictures of people/party food (some cut out in advance)

How it works
Give each child an 'invitation' to give to Jesus.

Dear Jesus,
Please come and have tea with me and be my friend.
Love ....

Help any children who can't write to write their name at the bottom. The children can then decorate the invitations with pens/crayons or with pictures cut out from catalogues of happy people/party food. (You need to have some of these cut out already.)

Talky bit
Before telling the story, you might want to explain the word 'saved' as meaning 'being made safe'.

Today's story is about a very small man, called Zacchaeus. Introduce the children to the doll/puppet you are using as Zacchaeus. The trouble was, he could never see over other people's shoulders, he was so small. But that didn't stop him making lots and lots of money. (Get doll/puppet to dance around with delight because of the purse of money – 'Ha, ha, I might be small, but I'm rich! Ha, ha!')

But, Zacchaeus had so much money because he had cheated, and taken more from people than he should have. So he was very unpopular, and had no friends. (Can anyone go 'Boo, boo, Zacchaeus is a cheat' . . . ?) So, he was small, rich but lonely. No one wanted to be with him.

But, one day he heard Jesus was in town and he decided to go and see him. (Use doll/puppet to think aloud 'Shall I go? . . . Shan't I go? . . . I think I will . . .'

Guess what, though – because he was so small, Zacchaeus couldn't see through the crowds of people that were also going to see Jesus. (Doll acts out: 'Let me see, push, push, out of my way, shove, push . . . Oh, it's no good – I'll never get

30

to see . . . *It's not fair!'*) Suddenly, Zacchaeus had a good idea. 'Hmm, what about if I climbed up that tree? . . . Then I could see . . .'

And that's just what he did. Just as he got up the tree *(get doll to climb up),* he heard a strong voice: 'Zacchaeus . . . Zacchaeus . . . come down . . . let's go and eat at your house.'

Well, Zacchaeus was amazed – and so were all the people. (*Children make surprised faces.*) They started to mutter: 'We don't like Zacchaeus . . . he's a cheat and has taken our money . . . ' (*Children mutter crossly to one another.*)

Then something even more amazing happened. Zacchaeus stood up and said in a loud voice: 'I'm sorry I took your money – I'll give it all back, and some extra, too. I really am sorry.'

The people were astonished (*children make suitable faces*), but Zacchaeus did as he said. Meeting Jesus changed him completely.

Ask the children to repeat the words of the verse after you, and explain that just like Zacchaeus, we can be saved from doing wrong things and be saved to be a friend of Jesus.

ACTIVITY 18

Royal puppets

I will serve God.
Joshua 24:15

You will need
- A sceptre (made from a cooking foil tube) wrapped in gold paper
- Wooden spoons or lollipop sticks
- Thin card for drawing faces of Esther, the king, Mordecai, Haman
- Scraps of material for puppet clothes
- Sticky tape for attaching material
- Small pieces of gold paper for crowns for Esther and the king

How it works
Make wooden-spoon puppets of the characters (alternatively, use lollipop sticks).

Stick the drawings of the faces onto the bowls of the spoons. Scraps of material can be gathered round their 'necks' and stuck/taped on. Crowns can be made for Esther and the king. These puppets can be operated by the children as you retell the story using the script below or retelling in your own words with your own dramatisation.

Talky bit
Esther was the new queen. She had just married the king. The king was very powerful. Everyone had to do just what he said. He sat on a great throne, wearing his crown and holding a golden sceptre. (*Take this opportunity to introduce the sceptre.*) Esther, too, had to do everything the king told her to do! She couldn't even go to see him or speak to him unless he told her to! She wasn't a powerful queen at all. (*You could talk here about fairytale monarchs they might know who do have great power, and can very easily make everything all right when things go wrong. Esther wasn't like them!*) But Esther was happy, and her cousin Mordecai was happy, because he knew Esther was safe.

There was a man called Haman who worked for the king. He was not a good man. He thought he was so important that people should do everything he told them to do. One day, Mordecai refused to do what Haman wanted him to do. Haman was very angry. 'I'm going to get rid of Mordecai!' he said. 'I know how to do it!' Now Mordecai and Esther were Jews, God's special people.

Haman went to the king. He told lies about the Jews, saying they were stealing money from the king. And the king believed him! He told Haman he could get rid of all the Jews. Now the king did not know that Esther, his beautiful new queen, was herself a Jew.

Mordecai told Esther that they and all their people were going to be killed. Esther didn't know what to do. She was very frightened. Mordecai said: 'Go to the king. Tell him we are not stealing from him. Tell him he must save us.'

But Esther said: 'I can't go to the king! If I go to see him when he hasn't told me to, he will have me killed immediately. I daren't do it!'

Mordecai said: 'This is our people's only chance. Perhaps this is why God has made you queen – so that you can save our people!'

So Esther decided she had to see the king. She asked all her people to ask God to look after her. She put on her best clothes. She walked down to the room where the king sat on his great throne. She knew that if the king held out the golden sceptre, it would show that he wasn't angry with her, and she would be safe.

The servants opened the doors and Esther walked in. She walked nearer and nearer to the king. She knew he had seen her coming. She reached the bottom of the steps leading up to the throne. She knelt down. What was the king going to do? Was he going to tell his servants to kill her for daring to come to him when he hadn't told her to? Or would he hold out the sceptre to her?

Everyone waited in silence. And then . . . the king held out the golden sceptre – and Esther knew she was safe. God had given her a special job to do – one that only she could do.

He had looked after her, and had helped her to be brave and to do that special job well. She told the king what Haman had been doing – and how he was trying to kill her people. The king was very angry with Haman. He made sure that her people were safe.

Explain what this means: Joshua was asking the people of God if they were going to follow God and do as he asked them to do, or if they were going to do what they wanted to do. He said he and his family were going to serve God. Explain that 'serve' here means to obey God, to find out what he wants us to do, and to do our best to do that. What did Esther want to do? What did she decide to do? What happened as a result?

ACTIVITY 19

Boxing clever!

But everyone who hears these words of mine and does not put them into practice is like a foolish man who built his house on sand.
Matthew 7:26

You will need
- Empty, safe cardboard boxes to build child-size houses (tape the lids down to form blocks for building)
- Seven inflated balloons. Using a thick felt pen write *Sorry* on three and *Thank you* on the others (these are for the conclusion)

How it works
Use the cardboard-box blocks and as you tell the story, the children can build the houses. One area of the room will be designated as sand, and the other as rock. It's good to have some extra helpers for this session, to ensure that stable 'houses' are built.

If you are feeling adventurous you could be creative by encouraging the inclusion of windows and doors, and felt tips can be used to draw bricks, tiles, door knobs, drainpipes, etc.

When the storm comes, the children can knock down the house in the sand area – safely, closely supervised by your extra helpers!

Talky bit
Talk about how the house built on the firm rock was safe, but the other one wasn't. Jesus told stories like this one to teach people something important. One of the things he was teaching in this story was about choices – about choosing things. The two men had to choose where to build their houses. One of them chose a safe place to live, the other chose a dangerous place.

Talk about our choices – how many of them chose what to eat this morning, or what to wear? How many of them chose a book for someone to read to them, or to look at by themselves? Talk about other simple choices they make every day. Grown-up people have even more choices to make. Some of them are just the same as the children's.

We all have some choices to make that are more difficult and more important. For instance, we have to choose how to treat other people. Talk about some of the ways in which we can treat others. Sometimes, it isn't easy to treat other people kindly, especially if they have not been kind to us! As we grow up, we have to make some really big decisions – such as where to live, what job to choose, whether to get married or not. These are like the choices the men had to make about where to build. We can make good choices that make us happy and keep us safe, or we can make poor choices, that make us, or others, unhappy, or put us in danger.

Jesus said that people who love him try to choose what he wants them to do. They ask him what he wants them to do, and they listen to him, and try to do it. It isn't always easy, but he will help us when we do this. If we try our best to do what he wants us to do, then, Jesus said we will be like the man living safely in the house built on the rock, because Jesus is like that rock – strong and firm. The rock didn't let the man down, and Jesus won't let down the people who follow him.

Say that when you make choices, and you know you have made the wrong choice, it's good to say sorry.

Invite the children to tell you some things for which they wish to thank God. Write these on three balloons. Use these to decorate the room. Ask them if any want to say sorry about anything. Write these on the other balloons, and then talk about God wanting to forgive us as soon as we say sorry, and how he has promised to forget what we have done wrong – as if it hadn't happened at all.

Check that you don't have any children who get upset by the sound of popping balloons. Once you know that's not the case, and having announced what you're going to do – burst the *Sorry* balloons (outside if necessary!). Show how you can no longer read the words. Remind them God has forgiven you, and has forgotten what you did wrong. Together, thank God for this, as you write it on the last balloon.

ACTIVITY 20

Prayer plant and self-portrait puppets

David and Goliath.
1 Samuel 17

You will need
- Lollipop sticks
- Thin card for drawing the children's faces
- Scraps of material for puppet clothes
- Sticky tape for attaching material

For a prayer plant you will need a drawing of a large plant with a few leaves, or some flowers with no petals.

How it works You can use lollipop sticks to make self-portrait puppets using the children's own drawings of their faces.

Use the material to stick on clothes for each puppet.

Use these to talk about and act out people standing up to their 'giants'.

Make a prayer plant. Use photographs or drawings of the children: paste each one onto a petal of a large flower. Write 'We pray for ....' in the centre of the flower. The children can then be prayed for or with in turn. This can be used in subsequent Sunday school sessions, but you'll need to keep it up to date with new children. To allow for this, spare petals can be incorporated at the beginning with other things to pray about – such as things to thank God for. Leaves can be stuck onto the plant's stem on which individual prayers can be recorded through the weeks.

Talky bit Summarise the story of David's feelings as he looked at the giant of a man confronting his people. Talk about things that might frighten us – but keep it impersonal. God helped David – and God will help us when we ask for his help. Point out that grown-ups face 'giants' too!

ACTIVITY 21

Special places game

He will wipe every tear from their eyes.
Revelation 21:4

You will need
- A washing line, an old sheet ripped up into handkerchief sizes, some clothes-pegs, and some felt pens. Rig up the washing-line, at a child-friendly height, but out of the way slightly so that no one walks into it!
- You'll also need some pieces of paper, each with one of the words from today's verse on them. Mix them up so that when you hand them out later they're not in the right order.

How it works
Hand out the 'handkerchiefs', and give out the pieces of paper with the words on them and, without the children knowing what other people have to write, get them to write the word they have on their piece of material.

When they've finished get them to hang up their 'hankies' on the washing line. Hopefully, the words won't be in the right order! You can say it looks as though there's a sentence there, but the words are all mixed up. Invite a couple of children to have a go at rearranging the words, but the others can help if they need it, by calling out instructions.

If more help is needed, tell them to find the text in the Bible (if someone hasn't already thought of doing so).

Then play this game – 'special places'
Before the session you will have placed big signs on the walls of the room or hall – these identify each of the walls as a special place – Home, Hospital, Playground, Bed.

You call out the name of each special place in turn and the group must run there as quickly as possible.

When they get there they must make the appropriate noise for where they are. So at home they will sit very quietly as if watching television or reading; in hospital they can groan as if in pain; at the playground they will start jumping on the spot as if they're playing hopscotch or skipping; and in bed they will lie down and make a snoring noise.

Give each player 10 lives and the last person to touch the wall each time loses a life. Don't play long enough for anyone to be 'out'.

Keep it moving quickly and at various points call out 'In the car!' at which point everyone sits down wherever they are and makes engine noises to signify that they're on the move to somewhere else . . . and then after a second or two continue by calling out one of the names on the walls.

Talky bit   Calm everyone down after the game by getting them to sit down quietly ready for a prayer time. Prepare for that by doing the following:

Arms out straight, wiggle your fingers! 'Wiggle, wiggle, wiggle.'

Fold your arms, count down together! '5-4-3-2-1'

Close your eyes, count down together! '5-4-3-2-1'

Bow your heads . . . let's pray.

Dear Heavenly Father,

We thank you that we can have fun in Sunday school. Thank you for our friends and games. Help us now . . . to not think about other things, but to concentrate on you.

In Jesus' name we pray. *Amen.*

Continue by asking if anyone has been upset this week. Be sensitive in any follow-up questioning, but show interest and concern.

It might be too much to expect your group to own up to shedding tears, but it's OK to say something like: 'Even though we're growing older, it's not unusual to cry when something upsets us.

Maybe some of you have cried this week when you were treated unfairly, or you might have cried when you hurt yourself physically. Grown-ups cry about things too, so it's not something to be ashamed of. Can you think of any times when you've been upset enough to cry? (At this point you might have someone say they cried when someone died. If not, you can point out that people often cry when someone dies.)

We're upset when we hear of the death of someone we really care about, maybe a member of our family or a close friend. God knows about our sadness.

The reason we're talking about these things this morning is so that we can think about a very special place that God tells us about in the Bible. He tells us that there's a special place for everyone he knows. It's heaven.

The Bible describes heaven as somewhere really good. It uses some lovely words to tell us what heaven is like. It talks about bright jewels, wonderful things to look at, and bright, shining lights, but best of all, it says that it's the place where we can be with God.

Listen to this description from the Bible:

I saw the Holy City, the New Jerusalem, coming down out of heaven from God, prepared as a bride beautifully dressed for her husband.

I heard a voice from the throne say: 'Now the dwelling of God is with men, and he will live with them. They will be his people, and God himself will be with them and be their God. He will wipe every tear from their eyes.'

The Holy City shone with the glory of God and its brilliance was like that of a very precious jewel, like a jasper, clear as crystal.

Now that sounds like the sort of place I'd like to be, but God tells us that not everyone will go to heaven. People need to decide for themselves whether they want to go there. God needs us to know Jesus while we're alive here on earth. While we live our lives we need to make sure that Jesus knows us. We do that by learning about him, talking to him, and listening to what he says to us.

ACTIVITY 22

The Good Samaritan (Luke 10)

Jesus said: 'The second most important commandment is this: "Love your neighbour, as you love yourself."'
Mark 12:31a

You will need
- An obstacle game: draw a 10 x 10 grid on card or paper (or use an overhead projector). Add the letters A-J along the top and the numbers 1-10 along one edge, to act as grid references. Decorate the grid, if you wish.
- Allocate hidden obstacles to some squares – these could relate to the journey in the story, e.g. 'Forgotten the way', 'Overcome by thirst', 'Robbers attack you', etc. Make a list of these, using the grid reference, e.g. A3, G8, etc., depending where you have put the 'obstacles'. The traveller has to make his/her way from one shaded square to another without encountering any hidden obstacles. Only reveal the 'obstacles' if they land on those particular squares. Try out the game with someone beforehand.
- A map, showing the location of Jerusalem and Jericho.
- Cue cards for the characters in the Good Samaritan story – copy the details below onto separate pieces of card or paper:

How it works
Play the obstacle game, possibly in teams, to see which team gets to the end of the course hitting the fewest obstacles. Move, possibly using dice – though it may be quicker just to allow each player to move three squares in any straight line. If an obstacle is hit, start over again. (Like a computer game, the children have to remember which way to move and which squares to avoid.)

Cue cards for the story characters
THE TRAVELLER:
   You are a bit reckless – willing to take risks. You know the road is dangerous, but you have to be in Jericho for a special occasion. You would normally wait until you could find a caravan of camels and traders going that way, but you could not wait. You did not carry any money, but the robbers still attacked you, and took your clothes and your shoes.

THE PRIEST:
   You know the road is dangerous, but you are sure that because you are a priest in the temple, and wear your robes, you might not be attacked. You were on your way to the temple, and when you saw the man on the road, you were afraid he was dead. If he was dead, and you touched him, you would be 'unclean' (according to the law) and unable to do your turn of duty in the temple for seven days (see Numbers 19:11).

THE LEVITE:

> You work in the temple in Jerusalem. You are not a priest, but you are supported by the offerings of pilgrims to the temple. You are quite wealthy, though you try not to show it. You know the road is dangerous, and that robbers often attack travellers. You know that one trick they use is to have someone pretend to be injured. Then, when someone stops to have a look, the rest of the gang leap out and rob them. Although you went near the injured man, you were not sure if it was a trick.

THE SAMARITAN:

> You are not actually a Samaritan, but you live there. You are a kind of commercial traveller, and you often travel this road on your donkey. You often stay at the inn, and the innkeeper knows you well. He can trust you to settle any unpaid bills next time you stay there. You know many Jews do not like Samaritans. They say Samaritans worship in the wrong place – a temple on Mount Gerizim 30 miles north of Jerusalem. They think you are wrong about other aspects of your religion, too. They think you are too friendly with pagans. But it doesn't bother you too much. You just want to be an honest trader, a good man, getting on with life.

Talky bit   Jesus was once asked which was the most important commandment (Matthew 22:36; Mark 12:28). His reply impressed his questioner. Ask if the children know the answer; if not, get them to look it up (or read it to them if they are poor readers). The religious authorities knew the law. Unfortunately, many of them did not do it as well as they knew it!

Talk about what loving God means – how do the children understand that phrase? Talk about loving our neighbour – the modern meaning of the word means someone who lives next door, and implies it is someone we know. But what about loving someone we don't know? Talk about that briefly, before introducing the parable.

Set the scene – show the children a map, showing Jerusalem – up in the mountains 700 metres above sea level. Jericho is near the Dead Sea, some 400 metres below sea level. The 20 mile road drops 1100 metres, winding and twisting through the wilderness. It was notorious for bandits, and so the story that Jesus told was not very unusual. If the children know the story, invite the children to act out a trial of the Samaritan – perhaps accused of being one of the robbers. Choose volunteers to be the characters in the story, and give them their cue cards to read as they prepare for the trial. They should not share the contents of the cards with anyone else at this stage.

When they are ready, call the characters one at a time into the witness box, and question them – why they did what they did, etc. You may wish to go for a verdict, but the cross-examination should be enough to draw out the facts.

Point to the important words of Jesus – 'Go and do as he did.' Talk about that. What can children do? In these days of stranger danger, how can children be safe and still help those in need? It may be by supporting a charity that works with needy people. It may be by standing up for those in school who get bullied or teased. Either way, to love our neighbour means it will cost us something.

ACTIVITY 23

Worthless containers

. . . though seeing, they may not see;
though hearing, they may not understand.
Luke 8:10

You will need
- Small pieces of paper or card
- Pens or pencils
- Envelopes or containers
- Sweets or some other small rewards

How it works Give each child in your group one or two pieces of paper or card, asking them to write their name on them. Place six or seven envelopes or containers around the room. One at a time, or perhaps as a kind of team game, invite the children to place their pieces in one or two of the containers, saying that some of the containers are more 'valuable' than the others, without indicating which. When they have done so, give each child some small treat (perhaps a sweet, though remember that not all children are allowed sweets). However, when you reveal the 'valuable' container(s), the children (or team) who put their papers in them should be given a small extra treat.

Talky bit Talk about the fact that if they had known which container(s) was more 'valuable', then all the children would have put their pieces of paper there. No one would use the 'worthless' containers.

In this week's Bible story, Jesus told of a farmer sowing seed. Some of the children will know the story, so allow them to tell it, and then have it read from St Luke's Gospel (Chapter 8). Relate the game to the story – the farmer would not deliberately sow his seed on 'worthless' soil. You could, perhaps, demonstrate the way the farmer would have walked up and down the field, taking a handful of seed from his basket and scattering it as he walked. That is why only 'some seed' fell on the different kinds of poor soil.

Ask what was more important to the farmer – it was of course, the seed that fell on the good soil, from which he eventually got a good crop – more seed to sow, and the rest to sell or make into flour for bread, etc.

Jesus said the seed was like God's message. Ask the children why that was so. Explain that people are like soil in which seeds are planted. Get four plastic plant pots. What kinds of people are like the different kinds of soil? The children can write the answers, or you can, placing them in the appropriate flower pot. Explain that God 'scatters his seeds' widely – he wants everyone to hear the Good News about Jesus (you may quickly explain that term, if the children do not know).

Each Gospel writer tells us that when Jesus told this parable (story with a meaning), it was when a large crowd gathered round him by the Sea of Galilee. He knew that his message was falling on different kinds of soil as he spoke. He knew that not everyone would do anything about it, and that some would be more fruitful than others.

The Gospel writers tell us a kind of mystery about the message. Read Matthew 13:11-12. A seed is alive – it can remain dormant for years and years, but still grow when planted in the right conditions of moisture and warmth, etc. The message about Jesus is alive, and can do things beyond our imagination. The more we give away the message, the more we will receive.

Talk about being fruitful – how do people who are good soil produce a good crop? You could talk about ways in which a farmer treats the soil to make it more productive. Ask the children in what ways can you, as their leader, help them to produce a good crop.

ACTIVITY 24

My plane's better!

Man looks at the outward appearance, but the Lord looks at the heart.
1 Samuel 16:7b

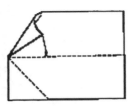

You will need
- A bucket or box
- Sheets of A4 paper – three for each child in the group, plus one or two for yourself

To make a paper dart:

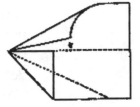

1. Fold A4 paper lengthwise

2. Fold corners in to middle

3. Fold new corners in to the middle

4. Fold over to centre

5. The result should be like the final line drawing on the right

- A picture of a Pharisee, a picture of a tax collector (see page 46)
- A set of kitchen scales – preferably the balance-type. Stick a label on the scales which says *Right with God*
- Five small boxes (matchboxes?) that can be stacked up on the scales. You may paint the boxes or cover them, but stick the following labels on them:
    Honest   Pure   Fasting   Tithing   Bad
- Add more weight to the *Bad* box, so that it weighs more than the other four together. (NB You could use shoe boxes and bathroom scales.)

How it works
Give each child three pieces of paper, telling them to write their name down one side. Place an empty bucket or box in front of the group. Quickly demonstrate a method of making a paper dart. Say to the children: 'When I say "go" make three paper darts and see if you can get them in the bucket/box, etc.'

They will be more concerned about scoring, but without telling the children, look for the best-made dart, and announce its maker as the winner. The wording you use is important, because you don't actually say the winner is the person who gets the most darts in the target.

There may, of course, be protests that you didn't say it was about making the best dart, etc. This will help you get into the Talky bit.

Talky bit   Jesus did not like those who looked down on others – people who think they are better than everyone else. He did not like it when his disciples began to argue about which one of them would be the most important person (Luke 9:46-48).

On this occasion, Luke tells us that Jesus was addressing a group of 'people who were sure they were right with God . . . who looked down on everybody else' (Luke 18:9). We don't know if they were Pharisees, but a Pharisee features in this 'story with a meaning' – parable. (*Show Pharisee picture.*)

Jesus often had confrontations with a group of people called Pharisees – 'The Separated Ones'. They were a religious party, many of whom were so concerned to keep God's law that they often seemed heartless. Personal opinion did not matter – what was important was keeping the letter of the law (that phrase may be new to some children, and you may need to explain it). They were not all bad, however, and some were followers of Jesus – Nicodemus being one example (John 3).

In this case, however, the Pharisee was like one of those Jesus often criticised. (If you wish, look up Luke 11:42-44; 16:15.)

The other person in the story is a tax collector. (*Show tax collector picture.*)

Tax collectors had few friends, because they were regarded as traitors (remember Zacchaeus in Luke 19?). They worked for the Roman authorities – the occupying forces. They were paid for the work they did, but they often became rich because they charged more taxes and duties than necessary, and kept the profit for themselves. No doubt they excused their behaviour as compensation for doing a job no one else wanted to do!

The two went to the temple in Jerusalem to pray. It was the only place for a tax collector, for they were barred from entering synagogues.

Read the story from Luke 18.

If you could weigh a person's deeds, then surely the Pharisee's deeds would weigh more and make him worthy of God's favour.

Go through the Pharisee's prayer, bearing in mind Jesus' description at the start of verse 11 – the man was not really praying – more boasting! (*Add the boxes to the scales at each boast.*)

Everyone would have agreed that the Pharisee was a very religious man who deserved God's blessing. (*Remove the boxes.*)

On the other hand, the tax collector would not even look up – he felt so bad about himself. He beat his chest (explain that this is a sign that you are very sorry – you don't hurt yourself as sometimes happens in other religions) – and asked God's forgiveness, for he was a sinner. (*Hold the Bad box, but don't put it on the scales, yet.*) This man had no chance of his deeds weighing heavy and deserving God's favour, but . . . (*now place the box on the scales*) Jesus said it was this terrible man, a traitor, who went home accepted by God – why? Because he was honest before God and admitted that he deserved nothing.

Help the children understand there was nothing wrong with the Pharisee's good deeds – it was his attitude that offended God. The Lord said to Samuel: 'Man looks at how someone appears on the outside. But I look at what is in his heart.' (1 Samuel 16:7)

Talk about pride and humility. Many Christians feel any kind of pride is wrong. Some even go as far as to say 'I can't do anything well', because they think that to say so would be pride. Ask the children when they think it is good to be proud and when it would be bad. There is a pride that is sinful, but not when a person's boasting acknowledges that it is because of God's goodness and help. If one really believes that, then we do not look upon ourselves as better than others, because God has no favourites (as our Memory verse states).

If appropriate, you may talk about the temple as the place where people found forgiveness on special occasions like the Day of Atonement (Yom Kippur). Christians believe that because of Jesus and his death on the cross (show a picture of the cross, if possible) we who deserve nothing can receive God's forgiveness at any time, and receive the gift of new life through the work of God the Holy Spirit (a gift and not a reward). Like the tax collector in the story, if we mean it, we can go home acceptable to God.

Memory verse
Man looks at the outward appearance, but the Lord looks at the heart.
1 Samuel 16:7b

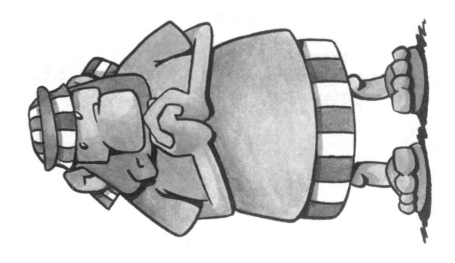

Tax Collector

Pharisee

ACTIVITY 25

Rules are rules!

You shall have no other Gods before me.
Exodus 20:3

You will need
- Black/whiteboard or flip-chart with chalk or pen
- A3 paper
- Glue stick
- A4 white paper (at least enough for three per child)

How it works
Play any simple game, e.g. noughts and crosses/hangman – but change the rules as you go along, or simply cheat.

When arguments start about keeping the rules, ask – is it fair to break rules? Why not?

Choose from the following suggestions:
Design a poster that could be put up at home or at school or around the shops illustrating any of the commandments. Think carefully about the wording. If there's time, choose another commandment – even make one of your own!

Start a book called *Rules* that can be continued in subsequent weeks. The posters produced on A4 paper could be stuck to A3 paper to form a large book or to be displayed in the church. Are these rules going to be positive or negative?

These could include:
Choosing another commandment and drawing a picture showing it in action today. Design a poster showing rules that they would like in their Sunday school group – e.g. we will sing at least three songs each week, or we will always have squash and biscuits at our meetings, etc.

Design a poster that could be put up at home agreeing certain rules, such as:
    I will always keep my bedroom tidy.
    I will not argue with my brother/sister, etc.

Talky bit
Use your imagination and describe the scene as Moses went up the mountain to meet with God. Talk briefly about the two tablets of stone, explaining what that means. Don't, however, go into so much detail that you leave too little time to look at the commandments themselves.

God gave us all rules for life when he gave them to Moses. What were they called? Write the numbers 1-10 on a board. Ask the children if they know any of the commandments and list them.

Read Exodus 20:1-17, using a child-friendly version of the Bible, and complete the list. Point out that you also find them in Deuteronomy 5:7-21.

Explain that God gave us rules in order that boys and girls, men and women could have happy, peaceful and rewarding lives.

Which rules are positive (do)? Which rules are negative (don't)?

Why are some negative and some positive?

Do the children know of any occasions when one of these rules has been broken?

Have they broken any of the rules? When? How?

Is it OK to break rules? (Whatever the answer – Why?)

Look at certain commandments; ensure you include: 'You shall not misuse the name of the Lord your God.' Whatever ones you choose ask the same questions.

What is God asking us to do? – is this easy? – why did he give us this rule? – would life be better without this rule?

ACTIVITY 26

Emotions towards others

As I have loved you, so you must love one another.
John 13:34.

You will need
- A4 plain paper and pencils
- Coloured pencils or crayons
- Felt pens
- Copies of the local paper
- Glue stick
- Ideas for a charity that your group could support

How it works   Explain that no one will see what the children write down.

Ask the children to write on a piece of paper a list of people they actually know and like (i.e. not famous people they have never met). Now write down a list of people they do not like. Once completed, ask why they like the people on one list and why they don't like the people on the other list. Which is the longer list? Is this significant?

Look together at the *Rules* book you started in Activity 25 (if you've already done it!). Perhaps the children could talk about the people they listed and whether they break the rules (without naming any names!).

Look through a local paper at articles about people who have helped someone else. Cut the articles out and stick them in the *Rules* book under the heading 'Love one another'. Write a short story about someone showing love to another person they don't particularly like. Illustrate it.

Design a poster to put up in your bedroom, to remind you that God wants you to love one another.

Talky bit   If your group does not support a charity perhaps they could think of a charity they could support. If it were a local charity it could be more relevant for the children. You could support just one person, e.g. a child who needs special equipment.

Come prepared with suggestions. How could you support that charity? List some ideas. Alternatively, the children might like to think about it in the coming week and return with suggestions on what (or whom) to support and ways to support it/them.

This is a perfect way of showing that you love one another, as commanded in this week's verse.

ACTIVITY 27

Follow the leader

Show proper respect to everyone.
1 Peter 2:17

You will need
- A4 plain paper
- Pencils
- Black/whiteboard or flip-chart with chalk or felt pen
- White or coloured card cut into the shape of bookmarks
- Cassette/CD player
- Copy of the Aretha Franklin song 'Respect'. Play this as the children arrive, or perhaps just before the Presentation

How it works
Give the children a series of instructions – e.g. move the tables and chairs, stand up, sit down, pat your head, shake hands with the person next to you, fold your arms, etc.

Afterwards ask why they followed your instructions. Explain that you are the leader and, hopefully, they will respect you and do what you say. You might like to get a child/children to give the group instructions, including the leaders.

All of us have to do what we are told by people in charge (or in authority over us) from time to time.

List on the board/flip-chart who the children think they have to obey, e.g. parents, grandparents, teachers, *Generators* leaders, police, club leaders, etc.

Why do they have to do what these people say?

We should do what these people say because we respect them and they should know what is best for us.

Also, you could:
Look at, and discuss, what was put in the *Rules* book in Activity 26.

On card, design a bookmark that has the words Respect Everyone on it. These could be taken home, placed in the *Rules* book, or used inside their Bibles.

If you are going to adopt a charity, now might be the time to discuss it more fully.

In the book you might like to put in the name of the charity. The children could work individually, in pairs or in groups, writing down how they could support the charity (getting information about it, what type of support, etc.). These ideas could be put in the book. In the *Rules* book write down any rules that they think appropriate, e.g. who should find the information, how often should they raise money, who looks after the money, who should write the letters to the charity, etc?

Discuss what you are going to do with the *Rules* book. Are you going to show it to people in church, other youth groups in your church, put it on display in the church or take it in turns to show it to people at home?

Talky bit Discuss if it is possible to show respect to people all the time. Sit quietly. Think about the times when you have been disrespectful to someone. How were you disrespectful? What should you have done?

Think about the times when someone has been disrespectful to you. How did you react? How did you feel? What should you have done?

In the quiet, ask God to help you – when you meet others – to respect who they are, and that they will respect you.

Or

The leader could say a prayer, use a prayer that one of the group has written, or use the following prayer:

Loving God,
    no matter how young or old we are
    there will always be people in authority over us.
Help us to respect that authority.
We also ask that those in authority will respect us.
Teach us to treat our family and friends with respect.

ACTIVITY 28

The building blocks of life

So if you think you are standing firm, be careful that you don't fall!
1 Corinthians 10:12.

You will need
- Jenga game or similar . . .
- Dominoes or Lego bricks.

How it works
The level at which this activity is undertaken depends on the time available and the number of children you have.

In a large group situation, play a game of Jenga. Divide the children into groups. You can have as many groups as you wish. One after the other each group selects a (different) child to remove a piece from the tower, i.e. all the children get to have a go. The game continues until the tower falls.

To make this activity more visible you might want to make your own large block version of the game. A stack of 20 blocks 4.5cm in thickness equals a tower nearly a metre tall!

Another large group alternative is to have two children race to construct a 'domino effect'. Obviously dominoes work best but if you cannot get any you can use any plastic bricks. Give each group 20 dominoes/bricks, which they must stand up, and knock down, in the time given. Try the 'four-length' Lego bricks. They will work as long as all the bricks face the same way when they are stacked up. You also need to ensure that when they are ready to be knocked down the children push the first brick on the side without any pimples (the side that would normally be the bottom when you are constructing something). At the end of the time given, the most complete run, or the first to finish (all bricks down) wins.

If you have a smaller group you could divide the children into pairs and they could all race each other. As the children are likely to be sitting down while completing this activity, have them stand up once they have finished. This way you will know who has 'won' and when everyone has finished.

Talky bit
Sit the children down and sum up this activity by talking with the children. Ask them why they thought their team won, or lost. Concentrate on the fact that they had to be careful and pay attention to what they were doing, all the time. One moment's carelessness and . . . disaster could strike.

Encourage the children to remain quiet before God and remind them that today's session has highlighted the need for us to be careful in our walk with God. Remind them of the strength that is gained by reading our Bibles and praying each day. However, we all know, and the Bible tells us, that we will make mistakes at some time or other – we will fall, we will sin. But what are we to do about it?

Now is the chance for the children to come before God and to ask for his forgiveness about the things that he put his finger on while they were worshipping.

In the quiet encourage the children to talk with God, as if they were talking to one of their friends.

Encourage the children to decide what they are going to do in response to God. If appropriate, get them to write down their course of action so they don't forget what they have said. Remember, the child might want to keep this confidential. Pray for them during this time, and with them if they want you to.

Take your time – there is no rush.

ACTIVITY 29

An 'apeeling' session

So I say, live by the Spirit, and you will not gratify the desires of the sinful nature.
Galatians 5:16

You will need
- One satsuma (orange) per child, *or*
  One chocolate orange
- Rubbish bags and cloths for cleaning up
- Twelve large balloons
- Two black plastic bin bags
- Marker pen (or computer-printed words)

How it works
No matter how large or small your group is, give each child a satsuma (orange). Let them peel it and eat it. Younger children might need help in peeling it – ask the older children to help them. Have rubbish bags and cloths for cleaning up ready and available. A handwipe each would be useful.

With a large group you could use a chocolate orange. Open and break it in full view of the children. Give a number of the children, perhaps those who are paying attention well, one segment each and allow them to eat it.

Once they have finished, sum up the activity by talking with the children about their satsuma. How did it taste? Is it good for them? Did they notice that the inside of an orange is made up of individual sections, different parts? Our lives are made up of many different parts too: school, home, at play, friends, church and so on. God wants to be involved in every part of our lives, not just on a Sunday for an hour or two. He wants us to put him first no matter what we do, where we go or who we are with.

Talky bit
Either write (in a thick marker pen) or type (a good, thick, bold font) each word of this week's verse on separate pieces of paper. If you don't have enough children in your group simply write more than one word on each piece of paper – the following instructions explain further.

You need to do this twice, once for each team. The pieces of paper must not be more than about 50mm (2in) wide, but they can be as long as you need.

Roll up each individual word/group of words and gently ease it into the neck of a balloon. Blow up, and tie off the balloon. As you do this the piece of paper will drop into the balloon. Once you have completed one set of balloons put those balloons into a black plastic bin bag. Tie this bag up and repeat the process for the second team.

This activity is a race. You will need two teams. Before starting the race each team needs to choose a team captain and as many team-mates as there are balloons.

On the command 'Go' each team rips open their bin bag. Each child takes one balloon, bursts it and finds the word(s) inside. Having found their word(s)

ACTIVITY 30

What would you do?

Make the most of every opportunity.
Ephesians 5:16

You will need
- A copy of *Find the fault* (page 56) – one per child
- Pencils – one per child
- A skipping rope
- Some pots and pans

How it works   Give each child a copy of the *Find the fault* sheet and let them complete it. Set up the following situations with the children and pose the question, 'What would *you* do?'

Situation one

Some of the children are playing skipping. Have three or four show you a skipping game that they know. Say that you'd like to join in, but you don't know the game; you've been told you're too big or too old to join in; and now you're feeling sad and lonely. Describe how, suddenly, the children remember that in Sunday school, their leader reminded them about a bit in the Bible that said 'make the most of every opportunity'. This is their opportunity to show God's love to the person who'd like to join in. What would *they* do? How could they make the most of this opportunity.

Situation two

There are pots and pans all over the place in the room (*scatter them about dramatically*). Have one of the children enter the room and start muttering things like: 'Look at the state of this place,' etc. After this has gone on for a few moments, and before doing anything else, tell the child actor to 'freeze'.

Ask the children if they can spot an opportunity. What would *they* do? Unfreeze the actor and encourage them to do what they think would take place if they were making the most of this opportunity.

Explain to the children that they can show that they have goodness inside them by serving. They can help out at home! Do the dishes, tidy up . . . surprise their family. What an opportunity!

Talky bit   Using a computer or marker pen write the words of this week's verse out on pieces of card – one word on one piece of card. Make the words as large and visible as you can.

On the reverse of each piece write the same word but mix the letters up. For example, the word *most* could become *stom*. Before the session starts stick the words of the verse on to a display board. Make certain the words are in the right order but with the mixed up side showing towards the children.

If you want to make the verse harder, simply mix the words up as well! The children not only have to work out the words but also in which order they should be.)

As you start this activity remind the children not to shout out an answer before they have been asked. Inform the children that you only wish them to tell you one word at a time, unless they can tell you the complete verse.

Ask the children to put up a hand if they think they can identify any one of the words. Choose one child and ask them which word they know. You will have to point to the words so that the others know which word they are identifying. Ask the child to tell you what they think the word is. If the child has answered correctly turn the word over and stick it in place, so that all the children can see what it says.

Continue like this until all the words have been turned over, or someone has correctly worked out the whole verse. Next have your group repeat the verse with you. Having removed one or two words, have them repeat it again. Repeat this process until all the words have been taken off your display board.

Finish off by saying that the *Find the fault* sheets were designed to show how it's often easy to spot something that's not right. Sometimes we look at our friends and judge what's not right in their lives, but it might be better to look at them and think about our opportunities to help them instead of criticise them.

ACTIVITY 31

Mime games – God speaks (1)

Then Samuel said, 'Speak, Lord, for your servant is listening.'
1 Samuel 3:10b

You will need
- Pieces of card with descriptions of simple actions – e.g. eating a '99' ice-cream; washing up grumpily; eating spaghetti messily; having a bad dream; waiting at a bus stop impatiently!; being annoyed with a brother or sister.
- Paper, pen and envelope for sketch.
- If possible find or draw some simple pictures to help with questions 4 and 5 in the Talky bit, i.e. someone sad; someone bored; someone walking into danger; something depicting the future; on one sheet of paper, an individual, a group of people, a church, a city, the world.
- Pictures to illustrate the story of Samuel as a boy and/or an interactive script of the story from *Play on Words* (available from Kevin Mayhew).

How it works   *'Get the message' mime game*

1. Divide children into two groups or teams and give three or four children from each group a piece of card with a simple action written on it. Ask them to take turns miming their action to the rest of their team who then have to guess what is being mimed.

2. Now use your leaders and/or one or two of the children to mime the following scene:
   X   Enters one side, sits down and looks sad, fed up and lonely. Freezes.
   Y   Enters opposite side, sits down, writes a letter, puts it in an envelope and then beckons Z to come and collect the letter and take it to X.
   X   Reads the letter and is much happier.

3. Question: What's going on?

Talky bit   Lead the discussion with the following questions. (NB Use the simple pictures you have prepared to illustrate the teaching arising from questions 4 and 5.)

Q1: What does a postman do?
   Establish that he is responsible for delivering letters – bringing messages. Introduce the fact that today we're thinking about prophets and prophecy).

Q2: What is a prophet?
   A prophet brings messages from God to people. A little like a postman. He's a messenger.

Q3: So, what is prophecy?
   It's the message we receive. It is God's word to us.

Q4: *What sort of message might it be?*
It could be a message –

(a) of encouragement and comfort.
A word from God that will make us feel loved, accepted, safe.
It might help us know what to do in a certain situation.

(b) of exhortation
That means it's a message that will stir us up, give us enthusiasm, make us excited about God and serving him.

(c) of warning.
Even a loving 'telling off!' (Give an example, e.g. the wise men warned in a dream not to go back to Herod.)

(d) Foretelling the future.
There are many prophecies in the Bible that have come true, but we will say more about this in another session.

Q5: *Who is prophecy for?*
A message from God may be for an individual, a group, a church, a city or a nation.

Q6: *Can anyone prophesy?*
God wants to communicate his word, his love, his encouragement to us and to the world. He is looking for people who will spend time with him, listening to him, learning more about him. In that way God will entrust us more and more with his messages both for ourselves and for others.

Reiterate the story (1 Samuel chapter 3) or read it from a suitable children's Bible, e.g. The International Children's Bible. If you can find some pictures to help with telling the story, so much the better. Alternatively (or in addition), use the interactive version in *Play on Words*, published by Kevin Mayhew (order via <www.kevinmayhew.com>

ACTIVITY 32

We're all ears! God Speaks (2)

Those who proclaim God's message help the whole church.
1 Corinthians 14:4b (Good News Bible).

You will need
- A collection of things that make a noise, with which the children will be familiar. Here are some examples: a packet of crisps; whistle; mug and spoon; mobile phone; tambourine; knife; fork and plate; squeaky toy; hairdryer; book; balloon (but don't burst it, instead rub something along its surface).
- Alternatively, make yourself a sound-effects tape. Record about 10 household sounds on a cassette and play them one at a time to the children. E.g. eating crisps, stirring a cup of tea, vacuuming, flushing the loo, boiling a kettle, the telephone ringing, an alarm clock and so on.
- Paper and pencils.
- If you're making sounds live, you'll need a screen or somewhere to hide while making them.
- Bean bags or soft balls.
- Bibles for the children to use.
- The following references written out on individual cards, enough for each group to have at least one reference. Luke 1:19; 2 Timothy 3:16; 1 Samuel 3:4; Acts 10:10; 1 Kings 18:1; Matthew 2:13; Jonah 1:1, 2; Acts 21:10, 11; Luke 18:1.
- Sets of six cards with the clues on one set, and the answers on another, as per the instructions later.
- Eleven small cardboard boxes (shoe boxes are good). Write one or more words of this week's verse onto strips of paper and stick these onto the sides of the boxes, not forgetting the reference. Number them.

How it works
Sounds game
Give the children paper and pencils, ask them to write down the numbers 1 to 10. Now hide behind a screen and make a noise with each of the objects and ask the children to guess the sound and write it down.

Alternatively, blindfolds could be used and individual children could take turns to be blindfolded and identify a sound. This could then become a team game.

NB Sounds can also be made like clapping, coughing, slapping legs, stamping, whistling, train noises, etc.

Memory verse game – Build a wall
Choose two children to come and build a wall or a tower with the boxes, which when built will spell out this week's verse. You could time them for one minute and then choose another two children and so on until the wall is built. The children will need to be told that box No.1 needs to be first/on the top, and the boxes with the reference last/on the bottom. The words need to be facing towards the front.

When built, read the verse together. Read the words of the verse alternately – girls then boys. Each time the children say a word they must stand, and sit when not speaking. Repeat until known.

A variation

Once the verse is learnt choose two or more children to come and throw bean bags or soft balls at the wall. Ask if it is easier and quicker to knock down the wall than to build it up?

Make the point that it's easier to discourage and hurt people with our words than to encourage and build up.

And another game . . .

Below are six facts about people who received a message from God. Write them onto pieces of card and number them 1 to 6 in the top left-hand corner.

1. He was told to go to Nineveh. (Jonah)
2. He said that there would be no rain for three years – 1 Kings 17:1. (Elijah)
3. He dreamt about the sun and the moon and the stars – Genesis 37:9. (Joseph)
4. They were told not to go back to King Herod – Matthew 2:11-12. (The Wise Men)
5. She was told by an angel that she was going to have a baby – Luke 1:26-38. (Mary)
6. He told his followers that the temple would be destroyed – Matthew 24:1, 2. (Jesus)

Now write the names of the people to whom these facts refer on a further set of six cards. Draw a geometrical shape in the right-hand corner of each card. Place these cards in a random order around the room. The children, using a Bible if needed, have to match up the fact with the person and write their answer in the shape.

Talky bit How does God speak?

The children will need to have Bibles.

1. Put the children into twos or threes and give each group one or more of the Bible verses above. If you have a large group it won't matter if some groups have the same reference (you could add extras yourself).
2. Explain to the children that the verses show us some of the different ways in which God speaks.
3. The children need to look up their references and decide how God is speaking – through a vision or audible voice, etc.
4. Give them a sheet of paper and when they think they know the answer ask them to draw a picture of it (like Pictionary).
5. When everyone has finished, each group can show their pictures and see if the rest of the group can guess what it means.

After each group shows their picture, say a little more about that particular way in which God speaks. Can the children think of any other times that God gave his message that way?

Give out the photcopiable sheet on page 63 to reinforce the session.

GOD SPEAKS THROUGH . . .

Angels: *Luke 1:19* – Angel Gabriel talks to Zechariah.

The Bible: *2 Timothy 3:16* – God speaks to us through Scripture.

An audible voice: *1 Samuel 3:4* – God spoke to Samuel.

Visions: *Acts 10:10-12* – Peter sees a vision of the sheet containing unclean animals.

Words: *1 Kings 18:1* – The Lord spoke his word to Elijah.

Dreams: *Matthew 2:13* – Joseph was told in a dream to flee to Egypt.

Other people: *Jonah 1:1, 2* – God sent Jonah with a message for the people of Nineveh.

An action: *Acts 21:10, 11* – Agabus and the belt.

A story/parable: *Luke 18:1* – Jesus used stories/parables to communicate God's message.

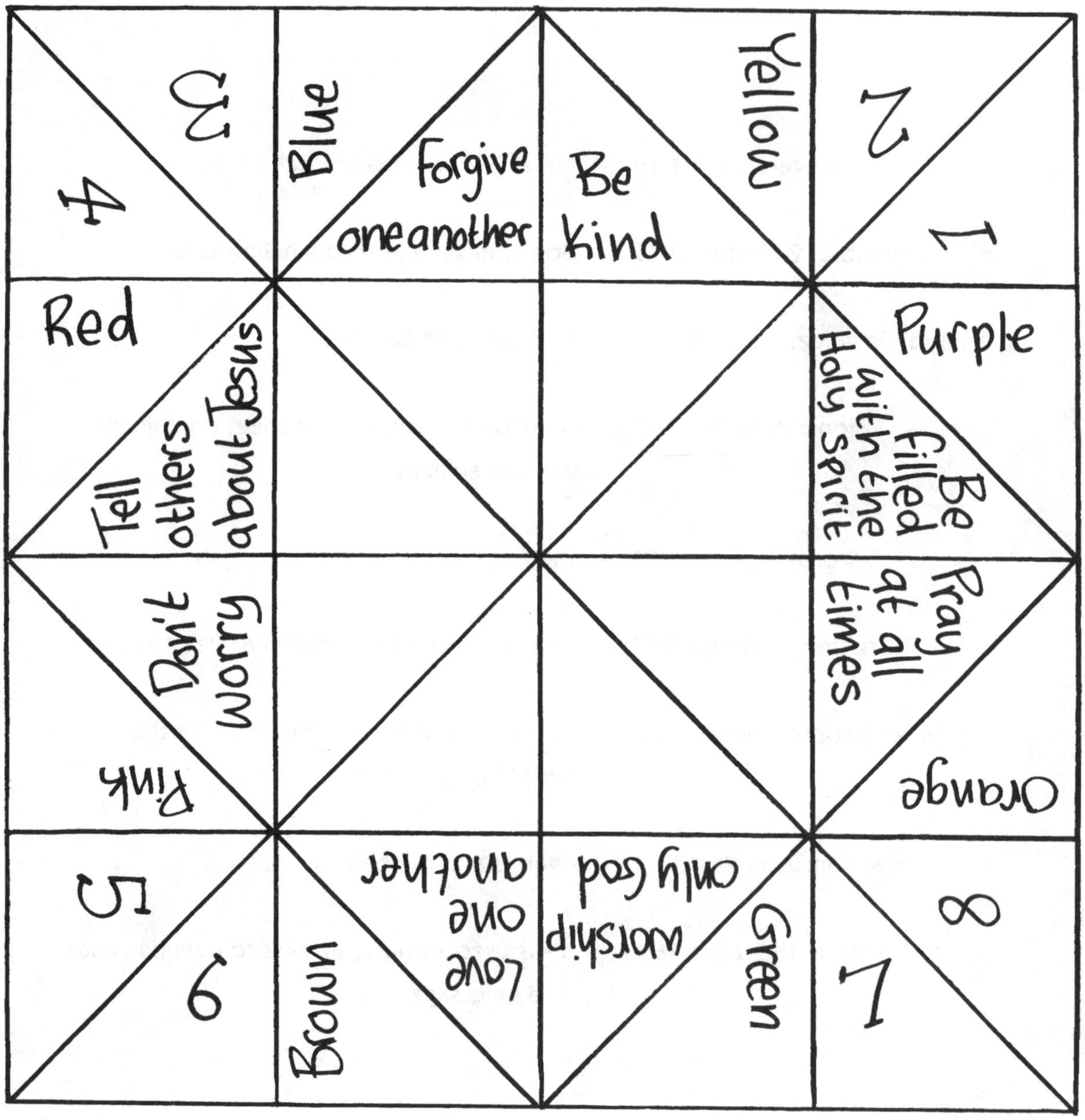

Red
Blue
Yellow
Purple
Orange
Green
Brown
Pink
1
2
3
4
5
6
7
8
Forgive one another
Be Kind
Be filled with the Holy Spirit
Pray at all times
Worship only God
Love one another
Don't worry
Tell others about Jesus

ACTIVITY 33

Bible command module

Now I know that you are a man of God and that the word of the Lord from your mouth is the truth. 1 Kings 17:24

You will need
- A wheelchair
- A blindfold
- Objects for an obstacle course

How it works
Have someone in a wheelchair be pushed through an obstacle course by a blindfolded helper. The one in the wheelchair has to give instructions to the pusher. The point of this activity is about guidance and listening to that guidance.

Many children will be familiar with the simple origami task (page 66) and so it can be a useful reinforcer, helping them learn and remember some of the words of encouragement we find in the Bible.

How to make it
- Photocopy the sheet opposite (page 64), sufficient for your group to have one each, and refer to the instructions on page 66.
- The 'colour' triangles may be coloured appropriately.
- With writing face up, fold diagonally, corner to corner. Open flat.
- Repeat for opposite corners. Open flat.
- Turn over so that the writing is face down.
- Fold each corner into the centre and crease (need to be as exact as possible).
- Turn paper over and fold each corner into the centre again.
- Now fold along the central horizontal line.
- Open and fold along central vertical line.
- Slip fingers under flaps to use.

How to use it
- Ask a person to choose a number as seen on top of the module.
- Next ask the person to choose one of the colours they can see.
- Spell out the colour name moving as before.
- Open the flap and read the command.

In addition to the sheet opposite, you could make one up with prayer reminders (e.g. family, church family, school, special people) and encourage the children to use it every day.

Talky bit
In the wheelchair activity, we learned to trust the person giving the guidance. We can learn to trust those who bring us God's messages.

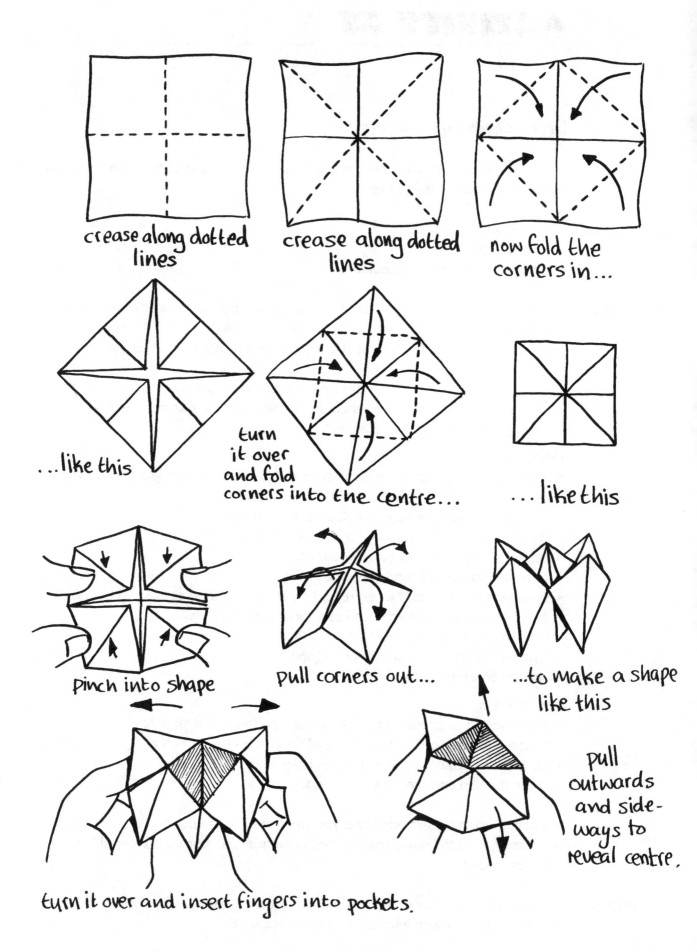

crease along dotted lines

crease along dotted lines

now fold the corners in...

...like this

turn it over and fold corners into the centre...

...like this

pinch into shape

pull corners out...

...to make a shape like this

turn it over and insert fingers into pockets.

pull outwards and sideways to reveal centre.

ACTIVITY 34

Visions galore

Your sons and daughters will prophesy, your old men will dream dreams, your young men will see visions.
Joel 2:28b

You will need Six objects or pictures, e.g. an unlit candle, an elastic band, a soft toy, a picture of mountains or water, a telephone, a piece of paper with a mark on it, a rechargeable battery, a torch, a glove, etc.

How it works Take the six objects or pictures and place them around the room. Ask the children, perhaps working in pairs, to look at each picture or object and think of something that God could be saying through each one. Explain to the children that today you will be looking at another prophet called Jeremiah, who often used objects or actions to bring God's message to people.

Tell the children that the verse is a prophecy about the time when the Holy Spirit was given, after Jesus went back to heaven.

Divide the verse into four sections (sentences) and discuss one at a time. What does this mean for the children? (That the giving of the Holy Spirit is to all believers, young and old, male and female, all classes, all nationalities.)

Give the children a brief outline of the prophet Jeremiah and the times when he lived. Tell them that the prophet Jeremiah and many of the other prophets who lived in his day were asked by God to do strange things. These are what we call 'prophetic actions' and involve doing something and not just speaking the message.

Use the following passages to teach the children about prophetic pictures and actions as seen in the Bible.

God speaks through pictures or visions
Jeremiah 1:13, 14
- Read Jeremiah 1:13 to the children.
- Tell them that this was a picture or vision that God gave to Jeremiah.
- Ask them if they think they know what it might mean.
- Read Jeremiah 1:14 – the explanation.

Be a visual aid!
It would be good if you or someone else (this may be someone who's not normally involved in children's ministry) could dramatise the Jeremiah prophetic action.

Actions speak louder than words!
Place a chair in the centre of the group.
Choose willing volunteers who will sit on the chair.
One at a time, whisper to each of the children something about the chair that will affect the way they sit on it.
After each 'sitting' ask the other children if they can guess what's going on.
  Here are some ideas:
  • The chair is sticky.
  • The chair is next to someone they don't like.
  • The chair has itching powder on it.
  • The chair is hard.
  • The chair is a throne.
  • The chair is broken.
  • The chair is smelly.

Talky bit *God speaks through actions*
Jeremiah 13:1-11
  • Read together the first five verses.
  • Explain to the children the significance of the linen belt in those days (The linen belt or waistcloth was quite a wide item of clothing that was worn close to the body. Linen was a material worn by priests and would have spoken of holiness. The fact that God told Jeremiah not to get it wet, also held significance. Normally this item of clothing would have been washed for it to become softer and more pliable and so this stiff linen belt was symbolic of the pride of the people.)
  • Ask the children if they have any idea why God told Jeremiah to do this. What do they think God's message was?
  • Read the remaining verses.
  • Check they understand the meaning, i.e. God said that he was like the belt that Jeremiah had worn for a while. It was as if his love and protection surrounded the people for a while but then, when they became proud and decided they didn't need him any more, it was like taking off the belt. Also, as they now worshipped other gods and did evil things, it was as if the belt got dirty and ruined and was good for nothing. God's love and protection became good for nothing to them.
  • This was a warning to change but the people didn't listen. In fact they were cruel to Jeremiah too and so, not long after this, Nebuchadnezzar, who was a very cruel king, came and attacked Jerusalem, killing many people and taking many prisoners back to Babylon.
  • Tell the children that Jeremiah performed a prophetic action – an action that brought a message from God.
  • Ask them if they can think of an action that would give a message. Give them an example first by putting your hands over your eyes as if blind and then remove them and look happy! This could mean 'you were blind and did not understand but now you see'.

ACTIVITY 35

Sword drill and card craft

For to us a child is born, to us a son is given.
Isaiah 9:6

You will need
- Bibles
- Lead (or clue) cards – one list for each group
- Evidence cards – write the reference and the verse on each card. Place individual cards in envelopes or other novel containers, numbered 1-5
- Paper, pens or pencils
- Small prize

For the Memory verse
- 14 stars with words of verse
- Display board (if used)
- Blu-Tack

For the card activity
- Templates of town scene and stars
- A4 yellow card, with the puzzle verse photocopied on one side
- Yellow, green, blue and black paint with a little PVA glue mixed in for thickness
- A star for each card (use gold or silver stars, if possible)
- Potatoes – cut into oblong chip shapes with a square end (approx. 1cm square)

How it works

Sword Drill

This game has been around for a long time, but if you have never heard of it, you play it as follows:

Tell the children to put their Bible under their arm (like a sword in its sheath). Tell them you are going to read out a Bible reference and then when you say 'Charge!' (and not before!) they must quickly draw their swords (open the Bible) and look up the verse. The first to find it stands up and reads the verse out loud.

Play this game using the following three verses from the Old Testament. After each one, the leader reads out the New Testament verses, which are the fulfilment of the prophecies.

Micah 5:2	(Luke 2:6)
Isaiah 7:14	(Luke 2:26-31)
Isaiah 9:6, 7	(Luke 2:30-33)

God told the prophet Isaiah about the birth of Jesus 800 years before it actually happened. This type of prophecy is called foretelling.

A Bethlehem Christmas puzzle card

NB: If using paint, this activity may need to be started near the very beginning of the session and possibly completed later in order to allow the paint to dry. Have one ready to show. An alternative would be to use pencil crayons instead of paint.

1. Photocopy a simple design onto yellow A4 card, one for each child, fold in half with the puzzle verse (below) inside.

> Th▲ L✚rd s✹ys, 'But y✚u, B▲thl▲h▲m
> Ephr✹th✹h, ar▲ ✚n▲ ✚f th▲ sm✹ll▲st
> t✚wns ✚f Jud✹h. But fr✚m y✚u w▼ll
> c✚m▲ ✚n▲ wh✚ w▼ll rul▲ Isr✹▲l
> f✚r m▲. H▲ c✚m▲s fr✚m v▲ry ✚ld
> t▼m▲s, fr✚m d✹ys l✚ng ✹g✚.'
> M▼c✹h 5 v▲rs▲ 2
> _____ 5 _____ 2

2. Open the card and write a greeting on the right hand page.
3. Place the template on the front of the card (nearer the bottom) and using the potato sticks and paint, stencil around the template. Start with yellow and stencil around the sides and top of the template first. Then gradually shade into blue and then to dark blue stopping just under the writing. (Make sure the children open out the card while they do this, because if the card is folded then some of the paint may seep out onto the inside.) Use green paint to potato print the bottom of the card.
4. When the paint is dry, add the star.

Talky bit *Bible verse game*

For to us a child is born, to us a son is given.
Isaiah 9:6

Mix up the 14 star cards with the words on them and spread them out on a table or on the floor (or Blu-Tack them onto a board). Ask the children to put them in the correct order to spell out the verse, putting the reference first.

Take the stars off a few at a time, repeating the verse each time, until you have removed all the stars and the verse is known.

ACTIVITY 36

Children tell the story

Let's have a feast and celebrate. For this son of mine was lost . . . and now is found. Luke 15:23b-24.

You will need
- Lolly/plant sticks – enough for two per child (plus spares if you make pig puppets too)
- Photocopies of main characters (two brothers and father) – and pig/pigs if you want to use them (page 72)
- Glue
- Colouring pens/pencils
- Sticky tape

How it works
Make puppets of the main characters – one puppet of sons – older on one side and younger on other; one puppet of father. Use the photocopiable resources below and make sure you have at least some of the characters cut out for those children who can't or won't be able to cut it out (give each child a photocopy of the four faces to take home). Stick the brothers back to back, and colour them in – and the father. Fix them to the short garden/lolly sticks. Retell the story using puppets, and encourage the children to act it out using their puppets.

Ask if anyone would like to relate the story to the group, using their puppets, while the rest of the group joins in. The fact that one of their own group is telling the story will be a very good way of reinforcing it.

Talky bit
Read the verse to the children – break it into three sections (perhaps quietly clapping a beat). Repeat a few times with the children. Keep it snappy.

Once the children are confident about the verse, underline its importance in the story . . . the fact that the father is overjoyed that his son has returned, and how the attitude of the father dispelled any anxiety the son had about coming home. If we do something wrong, although it makes God sad, he is happy when we come to him and say sorry. He will welcome us with open arms, just as the father in this story welcomed his son.

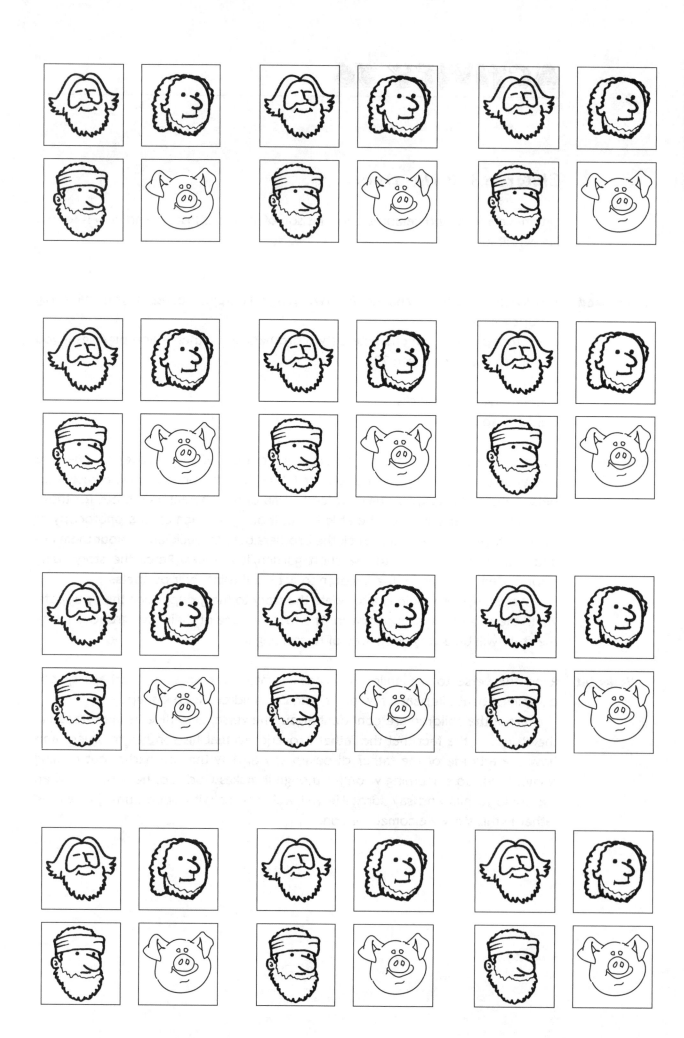

ACTIVITY 37

A giving game

Each man should give what he has decided in his heart to give . . . for God loves a cheerful giver.
2 Corinthians 9:7

You will need
- A tube of Smarties for each child
- Serviettes
- A treasure chest
- Wads of toy money
- Toy trumpets or similar
- Coloured pencils or felt pens
- Information from a charity
- Resources for poster making

How it works

Smarties party

In Old Testament times God asked his people to give him one tenth of everything they earned. The biblical word for this is to tithe. (Actually God asked for quite a few offerings from his people, but as many Christians today still find one tenth a helpful starting point, we'll stick with that.) Let's find out in a fun way what this would look like.

Give each child a tube of Smarties and a serviette. Tell the children that they will be allowed to eat the Smarties later but not yet. Ask them to tip the Smarties out onto the serviette and arrange them in lines of ten.

For each complete group of ten, move one a little distance away from the other nine. Those two or three would be your tithe, the ones God asks you to give away. The others are yours. Just look at how many you still have. If you had 20 pence pocket money, then your tithe would be two pence. What would it be if you had 50 pence, or 70 pence, or £1?

Ask the children to put their 'tithed' Smarties back into the box and to think of someone outside the group they could give those to after the session. Tell the children that the rest of the Smarties are theirs to keep or to share as they wish but don't forget to let them know when they can begin to eat them – either now or later!

It is worth saying that two pence, five pence, even 25 pence a week might not seem much but it is the principle that is important. God can take a little and turn it into a lot, as the story of the boy with the five loaves and the two fishes illustrates. What God wants from us is obedience.

Talky bit

Remind the group about today's verse. Can you work out some simple mimes or actions to communicate the words of the verse without using your voices? Having worked out the whole verse, mime it a few times all together. You could cover up parts of the verse and see if the group can still recite it correctly, and then cover up more and more until eventually they can recite it without any prompting at all. Remind them of any reward system you use for those who can still remember this verse next time.

It can aid people's giving if they are asked to give to a specific and manageable project. For example, a tube of eye ointment costing £1.50 could stop a person in India from going blind. Are there currently any such initiatives in the news or from charities with which your group could get involved? Could you set a realistic target for yourselves? Could you, for example, buy 20 tubes of ointment by Christmas?

If so, could you do something to raise awareness of this issue in your church or meeting area? For example, you might:

- produce posters to advertise the initiative
- put up a display of ready-produced material from an organisation like TearFund
- organise a cake sale over coffee after the service in the next couple of weeks with the proceeds going to this work

Discuss this with the children and see how enthusiastic their response is. A letter to carers or parents will keep them informed and improve communication between you, the group leader, and them.

This short, dramatised reading will work well and with a little organisation you can involve the children.

Mark 12:41-44
You could read this passage from the Bible together and then act it out:

(Jesus is sitting to one side of the stage; the disciples are nearby. A chest occupies centre stage and there are a selection of bystanders scattered around chatting to one another in twos and threes.)

Narrator One day when Jesus was in the temple he sat down near to where people were coming to put their money into the temple treasury.

Rich person 1 (*Makes a loud entrance, greeting everyone around as he arrives.*) Good day, good day to you my friend. Yes, I'm here again to give my offering to God. (*He gets a wad of notes out of his wallet and tosses them in the direction of the treasury chest. Bystanders are impressed and gasp in approval.*) I think he should be pretty pleased with me today, ha ha. Well, I'd better be off, places to go, people to see, don't you know?

Rich person 2 (*Trumpeters sound his arrival. Everyone turns to look. He sweeps in, straight up to the chest, then turns to make sure everyone is looking. Satisfied, he makes a great show of placing lots of money into the chest. Turns on his heel and sweeps out again. Bystanders bow or nod approvingly.*)

Rich person 3 (*The falsely modest one. He makes a quiet entrance but still manages to draw attention to himself as he stands at the chest.*) Oh dear, I hope no one is watching me. I haven't got much at all to put in today, just an odd bit of loose change. (*He proudly drops several wads of notes into the chest and leaves.*)

Narrator As Jesus continued watching, a poor old widow shuffled forward from the crowd. Nobody paid much attention as she placed two tiny copper coins into the treasury chest and shuffled off again.

Jesus Peter, James bring the others over here a minute will you? (*The disciples gather round.*) Did you see that poor old widow put her offering in?

Peter I did. She didn't put much in, did she, Lord?

Jesus I tell you the truth, Peter, she put more into the treasury than all the others.

Disciples (*Puzzled looks.*) Eh? What do you mean, Lord?

Jesus Well, those rich people have masses of money, and even though they put a lot in to the offering they still have piles of money left. On the other hand the old widow doesn't have much at all and yet she put in everything she has to live on.

Peter Wow! I get it now. She put in more than anyone. That's amazing!

Jesus Well done, Peter. You've got it. Come on, it's time we were going.
(*Jesus and the disciples walk off.*)

Discuss with the group the issues raised in this story. Starting points could be:
- Why did Jesus praise the woman's giving?
- What differences did you identify in the attitudes of those who came to give?
- Did Jesus attach importance to the amount each one gave?

Think about what we can learn from this about our giving.

ACTIVITY 38

Mission awareness

How awesome is the Lord Most High, the great King over all the earth!
Psalm 47:2

You will need Set the room up as follows:
- Streamers of colours based on the national flag of a country where you or your church have missionary connections
- A display of pictures and articles from the country
- Some music from this country playing in the background while children arrive
- Some appropriate snacks or finger foods from your chosen country
- 20 small items connected with the country of your choice, arranged on a tray, with a cloth to hide them from view
- Bibles
- Cassette recorder or means of recording an mpeg message on a computer
- A plimsoll and a bread roll

How it works Arrange the 20 small items connected with your country on a tray – they may be ornaments, products from the country you can find in the supermarket or market, a Bible in the native language, a doll in national costume: anything you like.

Give the children two minutes to sit and look at or handle (if appropriate) the items on display. Then cover the items over. Ask the group to work in pairs and list as many of the objects on the tray as they can. After five minutes bring back the tray and talk through the items as the children tick off their answers.

The winning pair is the one with the most items listed.

Talky bit Introduce the country with which you have contact and show pictures of the people working there whom you know (or describe their family circumstances). Explain that they are working for God.

When you have described all the above, explain how important it is for the people working in this way to receive support from home – not just money, but letters, e-mails, phone calls, text messages, etc. Ask if the group would like to put together a tape to send to them and/or to any children in the church where they're working. It could include personal messages for your friend or for the children, some songs recorded while your group are worshipping or anything else that seems relevant.

Bible input
Read Matthew 28:18-20 together, and then get the children to work in pairs to answer the following questions.
1. Who is Jesus speaking to?
2. Where does he send them?

3. What two things does he ask them to do when they get there?
4. How does he encourage them as they go to do his work?

Talk through the answers as a whole group and sum up this part by getting the children to understand what this means for us.

What implications does this have for us and for Christians worldwide as followers of Jesus in the twenty-first century?

We also have to obey Jesus' command to go and make more followers of him.

For some of us that may mean going to another country at some stage in the future; for others of us it may be moving somewhere else in this country; others will stay right where they are. But all of us have been commanded to share the good news of Jesus with others and ask them to follow him, too.

How we do that is not really what we're focusing on today, but we can look at this in more detail in a future session.

Show the children a plimsoll and a bread roll. Ask the children what they call each of these things. Has anyone ever come across other names for these items?

People in various parts of the country have different names for rolls: a cob, a batch, a bread cake, a stottie, a barm cake and so on. Similarly, plimsolls can also be known as pumps or sandshoes. In both instances people are talking about the same thing, although they use different words. Which words they use simply depend on where in the country they happen to live.

Throughout the ages and in many and various parts of the world people have come to faith in the Lord Jesus. The truths of the Gospel are the same the world over. However, sometimes the ways in which people express that faith and the ways they worship can be very different in different parts of the world. It isn't that one way is right and another way is wrong but just that people from different cultures will worship differently. God's word asks us to worship him in spirit and in truth and as long as that is what we are doing then God is pleased with our worship however it is expressed.

Closing game – Hangman
How awesome is the Lord Most High, the great King over all the earth!
Psalm 47:2

Play the game of hangman as a means of learning the verse. If you are short of time you may want to put in some letters, for example some or all of the vowels.

Depending on the size of your group you could either let the children work individually or alternatively you could split them into two teams. One person from each team suggests a letter on each turn and the winner is the first individual or team to be able to recite the whole verse and reference correctly. If you choose to play this in teams then the whole team has to be able to recite the verse together correctly before the winner can be declared.

It is good then to have all the children say the verse together several times, both with the words in front of them and then without the words to prompt them.

ACTIVITY 39

'Eat your words' Bible game

How sweet are your words to my taste, sweeter than honey to my mouth!
Psalm 119:103

You will need
- A selection of different kinds of books for the game, or two copies of each if you are doing it as a team game: A-Z type map book, world atlas, story book, telephone directory, dictionary, cookery book, hymn/song book, gardening book, DIY book, Bible
- Small items such as sweets to give as rewards to game winners
- Materials for the craft project if you decide to do one
- A group scrapbook, bought or made up
- Paper, pens, etc. for writing favourite Bible verses, or drawings and pictures of Bible stories
- Crispbread biscuits and squeezable honey (plus wipes)

How it works

The library game

If you want to organise this as a team game split the group into two equal teams. You will need two of each of the following types of books – they don't need to be identical but it would help if there were pictorial clues on the covers to help poorer readers:

Map book, atlas, story book, telephone directory, dictionary, cookery book, hymn/song book, gardening book, DIY book, Bible, etc.

Either spread the books out in front of the children in the group or spread the books out on two tables at the back of the room – one table for each team.

Ask one child from each team to listen to a clue and then to run to their team's table, find the book you have asked for and race back to the front with it. Award points to the team whose runner is the first one back with the correct type of book. Try one example first to make sure that all the children know where to run and what to do.

Bring me a book in which you would find:

1. A motorway – Map or atlas
2. The recipe for bread – Cookery book
3. The meaning of a word – Dictionary
4. A song to sing – Hymn book
5. A phone number – Telephone directory
6. Australia – Atlas
7. How to plant a rose – Gardening book
8. A story about Jesus – Bible

9. How to put up a shelf – DIY book

10. A bed-time story – Story book/Bible

11. How to plan your holiday – Map book or atlas

12. How to spell a word – Dictionary

Other questions could be asked depending on time. Remember to have a tie-breaker question up your sleeve if you are doing this as a team game and some sweets or other small prizes for the winning team.

Something to make

1. Giant Bible poster/collage

   Get the children to make a large picture together of their favourite Bible stories on a giant background sheet cut into the shape of a book.

2. Bible Bits book

   Make up a scrapbook or display with special Bible verses that the children have learned as a group. The children could well be surprised to discover just how many verses they have got to know over the years. They could also ask friends and relatives to tell them about their favourite Bible passages, and they could then illustrate the passages with drawings.

Talky bit *Eat your Bible!*

In Jewish synagogue schools one way in which boys were taught to love the word of God was to write parts of it on their slates in honey and then lick it off again. You could give your group the opportunity to have a go at this by writing a word or two from Psalm 119:103 on a crispbread using squeezable honey. Put them all together to learn the verse and then lick them. Have some baby wipes available for afterwards!

ACTIVITY 40

Our Bible

Your word is a lamp to my feet and a light for my path.
Psalm 119:105

You will need *Pass the parcel game*
A parcel made up with a central present which should be a bag or packet of sweets containing enough for everybody to share, and should have a label attached which says 'For the whole group to share' and a single sweet between all the layers of wrapping paper.
A CD or tape player and lively music.

How it works Play a game of pass the parcel. Prepare the parcel as explained above. Make sure that everyone gets at least one turn to take off a layer of paper. Allow the children to eat their sweet as they take it out of the parcel but when they get to the big prize tell them that they will have to wait until you say they can have it some time later in the session.

After the game talk briefly about the fact that some people only had to wait a short time for a sweet, while others had to wait longer, and of course we're all still waiting for the last prize. Today we're going to hear a story about a girl who had to wait for a really long time for something she wanted.

Talky bit *Story*
About two hundred years ago in a small cottage in Wales there lived a mother and a father and a young girl named Mary Jones. Mary probably had brothers and sisters living with her too. Mary's father was a weaver who made cloth from sheep's wool to sell at the market, and Mary's mother looked after the house and the family and helped her husband with the weaving. They were quite a poor family and everyone had to help: Mary had her jobs to do too. But at night when the day's work was all done everyone would gather round the fire to listen to stories. Sometimes Mary's father would tell them exciting stories about famous people and their adventures: at other times he would tell them wonderful Bible stories about Noah and Joseph, David and Daniel and especially Jesus. These were Mary's favourite stories.

Although Mary loved to hear the Bible stories she was not happy. She wanted to be able to read the stories for herself but she could not read and neither could her mother and father and there was no school in Mary's village where she could go to learn to read. It seemed hopeless.

'Never mind,' said Mary's father when she talked to him about it. 'If you listen carefully in chapel you will soon learn the stories for yourself just like I did. And anyway even if you could read we could never afford to have a Bible of our own: only rich people can do that.'

Mary was very disappointed but still she dreamed of being able to read her own Bible. Then one day she heard some exciting news. A school was going to be opened in the village near to where she lived! Mary would have to walk two miles to school and two miles home again but at last she could learn to read! She was thrilled and happily said 'Thank you' to God for her new school. She listened well and worked hard at her lessons because she was so eager to learn to read.

Not far from the cottage where Mary and her family lived there was a big house where Farmer Evans and his family lived. They were a rich family who owned a Bible of their own. Sometimes when Mary visited Mrs Evans she allowed Mary to touch the Bible and hold it for herself. Then she would read Mary a Bible story. Mrs Evans very kindly told Mary that when she had learned to read she could come to the house to read the Bible for herself. Mary was delighted and after some while she got good enough at her reading to be able to read the Bible for herself. The first part of her dream had come true but still she dreamed of owning a Bible of her very own.

Mary could have given up but then one day when she was ten years old Mary decided that she was going to save up every penny she could until she could afford to buy her own Bible.

'It's going to take you a very long time' her father told her. But Mary was determined. She did her chores in the house and then when she was free she did jobs for other people. Every penny she earned went into a special money box that her father had made for her. From time to time Mary would take the coins out and count them. Finally after six long years the wonderful day came when Mary had earned enough money to pay for her Bible. By now Mary was sixteen years old.

Mary found out that she could buy a Bible from a man in Bala called Mr Charles. Bala was 25 miles away from where Mary lived but she didn't let a little thing like that stop her. One morning she set out from her home to walk all the way to Bala to buy her Bible. But when she got to Mr Charles there was great disappointment. He only had three Bibles and they were all promised to other people! Mary was heartbroken. When he saw how upset she was Mr Charles said 'Sit down Mary. Dry your eyes and tell me all about it.' When he heard Mary's story of how hard she had worked, how long she had saved and how far she had walked for her beloved Bible he spoke to one of the other people who was going to have a Bible. They agreed to let Mary have their Bible and to wait for the next delivery for one of their own. So the next day Mary walked 25 miles home again proudly clutching her Bible. Soon she was sitting round the fire with her family in the evening delightedly reading the Bible to them all and giving thanks to God that her dream at last had come true.

We might never have known about Mary Jones if it hadn't happened that a few months after Mary had been to see Mr Charles he was invited to speak at a big meeting. He was asked to tell the people about the need for more Bibles in the Welsh language and so he told them Mary's story. The people at the meeting decided that there must be many more people like Mary around the world and so they formed a special group called the British and Foreign Bible Society. They wanted to help by providing Bibles for as many people as possible around the world. They wanted the Bibles to be in people's own languages and at a price that ordinary people could afford.

That group was formed nearly 200 years ago and since that day parts of the Bible have been translated into more than 1800 different languages!

ACTIVITY 41

Word games

The grass withers and the flowers fall, but the word of our God stands for ever.
Isaiah 40:8

You will need
- Pencils and paper
- Possibly a CD or tape player and lively music
- Some pre-prepared cards each with a different Bible verse (of similar lengths) written on them
- A large board at the front of the group (blackboard/whiteboard or flip-chart)
- A selection of 'communication cards' with words which are connected with communication, for example, pen, book, scroll, telephone, television, mobile phone, shouting, letter, message in a bottle. The children will have to communicate these words by drawing pictures

How it works
Game – Bosses and secretaries
If you have a space for your own group split the children into pairs, and have one of each pair take a pencil and paper to the far end of the room. These children are the secretaries. The other children are the bosses, and they remain with you at this end of the room. Give each 'boss' a verse from the Bible, choosing different verses of similar length for the different bosses.

When you say 'Begin!' all the bosses start to read their words as loud as they can to their secretaries who must try to write them down. With several bosses all shouting at once it will probably be easy to be confused but if you think that the confusion may need a little help then you could add in some fairly loud music!

At the end of the game the pair that communicated their message most accurately are the winners. Have some small prizes available. (Be careful with the level of literacy of your children, as some may be excellent at reading and writing but others may still be finding it difficult. Spelling is unimportant in this exercise.)

Game – Picture words
Using the 'communication cards', get children or leaders to draw the item or action as quickly as they can on the board in front of the group, while the rest try to discover what the word on the card is. The winner of one round is the artist for the following round.

You could play this in two or more teams who will need to communicate with each other very quietly so as not to help their opponents. The winning team is the one to get through the whole list first.

Talky bit
Words are very important. They can be used to lift people up, but sometimes they can be used to knock people down.

We are called to spread God's word throughout the world. That might sound like a big challenge, but we can start right where we are, with our friends and our family.

To reinforce what you've said, have the children act out the Bible verse, as follows.

Line 1 *Though the grass may wither*
The children begin standing but then sway and shrink until they are kneeling upright on their knees.

Line 2 *And the flowers may fall*
The children wave their arms to symbolise flowers and then bend over with their hands and faces close to the floor.

Line 3 *The word of the Lord*
Children kneel up again with hands held together in front of them like a book.

Line 4 *Shall stand for ever*
Children stand on their feet and move hands and arms wide.

ACTIVITY 42

'Where's Zacchaeus?' game

For the Son of Man came to seek and to save what was lost.
Luke 19:10

You will need
- Zacchaeus shapes (a small man). Make sure there are enough shapes to write the verse on (one word at a time) for each child
- Write one word from the verse onto each Zacchaeus shape and colour code each set so that one child will collect, say, all those shapes with a red spot in the corner and another will collect the blue ones.
- Use shapes cut from a magazine (for camouflage) or plain white paper, just to give a little mystery and added tension to the activity.

How it works
Hide the Zacchaeus shapes around the room. Allow a short time to find all the shapes and rearrange into the verse. Children should collect different words and then try and make a sentence. Finish the activity when two or three children have completed the verse correctly.

Talky bit
Tell the story of Zacchaeus (Luke 19:1-10) in your own words or using a children's Bible as an expressive reading.

Explain that many of us feel like Zacchaeus and want to be noticed. Many may feel that they aren't worth much or could never be important to God. This passage should point out to everyone that no matter how we or others view us, we are very special to God. Add other verses that will point out how wonderfully we are made (Psalm 139) and how God loves us so much he was willing to die for each one of us.

It's always good to remind the children of John 3:16 and the message that conveys.

As a direct response to hearing about how much they mean to Jesus, children can say their own prayer either aloud or silently. They can say simple 'Thank you' prayers if they feel this is for them. They can admit the times they get lost and do the wrong thing and they can ask forgiveness from God. They can ask for God's help to do the things he would want them to. By seeing your confidence is 'talking' to God, children are encouraged to pray. Taking turns by 'passing' a prayer around a circle is a good way to give everyone an opportunity to pray, or let a prayer pass on by. Pass an object from person to person to indicate whose turn it is, or hold hands and squeeze the next person's hand to signify passing on, or even just touch the next person when the prayer is finished.

ACTIVITY 43

Heaven is a wonderful place

Jesus said to her: 'I am the resurrection and the life. He who believes in me will live, even though he dies; and whoever lives and believes in me will never die.'
John 11:25

You will need
- Magazines containing colour pictures of scenery that could be used to convey an idea of heaven. Be adventurous and imaginative. Your young people's idea of heaven might be different to your own, so maybe pictures of funfairs or theme parks, football stadia, burger bars etc., would be appropriate!
- A4 paper, safety scissors and glue
- Newspaper front pages (suitable publications) so that the children can copy the layout style for their own front pages

How it works
Talk about heaven (as described in the Bible), as being a place where there will be no more tears, or sadness. Ask for some ideas of what their idea of heaven would be. Show some magazine pictures of beautiful scenes. Allow time for the group to cut out and stick down their own collage of 'heaven' pictures. Encourage discussion, through you as leader, to talk about the children's concept of heaven. Allow a 'show and tell' time for sharing the images of the collages.

Read the story of Lazarus in John 11:1-45 from a suitable children's Bible and dramatise the story if possible with adult helpers who could dress up and mime the story as it unfolds. Encourage your helpers to dress appropriately.

Talky bit
At the beginning of this part of the session explain to the children about the passages in the Bible that tell of meetings that Jesus had with many people and how their lives were always changed by meeting with him. When Jesus is around, all sorts of things can happen that seem different. In this case Lazarus was brought back to life and that's something that everyone would remember. It certainly meant something very special to Lazarus.

Hold the front page!
Suggest that in pairs, the children design the front page of a newspaper, or work out how a reporter might appear on a news bulletin such as *Newsround* and report the incident. One of the children could be an 'anchor' back in the studio while another provides an eyewitness report.

It might be difficult for some to believe that Jesus could heal Lazarus. It might be difficult for them to grasp the idea of heaven but after the activity and discussion time and after hearing about Lazarus, some might be curious to find out more. Some might want to know how to believe in Jesus, or they might want to ask Jesus into their lives. Spend time discussing this and, if appropriate, continue on to a prayer of commitment or thanks. As a direct response to hearing about Jesus, children can say their own prayer either aloud or silently. They can say simple 'thank you' prayers if they feel this is for them. They should be encouraged to be as spontaneous as possible. Leading a prayer by saying a short sentence and then allowing everyone to repeat the words can help hesitant children. This point has been made before, but by seeing and hearing your confidence in 'talking' to God, children will be encouraged to pray.

ACTIVITY 44

'I can do that' autographs

I can do everything through him who gives me strength.
Philippians 4:13

You will need
- Photocopied autograph sheet for each child, with the following statements and a space beside each for a signature (autograph); pencils
  - I can ride a bike
  - I can knit
  - I can sew on a button
  - I can write with my left hand
  - I can type
  - I can tap dance
  - I can say the alphabet – backwards
  - I watch *Coronation Street*
  - I don't like ice cream
  - I am good at headers in football
  - I help to walk my dog
- Add other categories relevant to your group, based on your knowledge, making sure there are ones that mean the youngsters have to ask an adult for their autograph

How it works
Give out the photocopied autograph sheet along with a pencil for each person. Allow time for everyone to try and get as many different autographs as possible. At the end of the time draw the group together and see who got the most different autographs and who could do the most 'unusual thing' on the list.

Talky bit
The autograph sheet activity will have helped the children discover things about each other that maybe they didn't know. They might even have found out something interesting about you, their leader, or some of the other adult helpers!

Encourage the children to acknowledge that they are special to God and to develop a trusting relationship with him in all that they do. Remind the children that God will equip and enable them to do things that he wants them to do . . . things that will be pleasing to him.

Since you have already spent time discovering things about each other, this is a great opportunity to continue your pastoral work with the group. There can never be too much time spent getting to know them and building up their trust. The world can be a very scary place for children of this age. So take time to talk about what has happened over the last week. Set a good example by listening carefully to each child and promoting a listening atmosphere where youngsters can feel confident to share things, knowing they will not be made fun of and are treated seriously.

ACTIVITY 45

A moving experience

You will be blessed if you obey the commands of the Lord your God.
Deuteronomy 11:27a

You will need
- Prepare a selection of 20 pictures of different household items (e.g. bed, iron, clothes, curtains, fridge, washing machine, clock, settee, etc.) cut from magazines, mounted onto individual pieces of card and numbered 1 to 20 (old Argos catalogues are excellent for a good source of pictures).
- Alternatively mount these onto A4 pieces of card with four or five pictures on each, making sure that each picture is clearly numbered and that the children can access them easily. *(NB When preparing these, remember that if you intend to use the given clues below you will need to make sure that you have included the pictures to which they refer.)*
- Photocopy sufficient lists of clues for your group to have one each.
- Before the children arrive Blu-Tack the pictures around the room.
- When you are ready to play the game, give each of the children a list of clues (the children could work in twos if they prefer).

How it works
The children need to solve the clues, find the picture of that item and record its number next to the appropriate clue on their paper. The first child or children to complete their list correctly wins. A small reward may be given to the winners.

Sometimes I'm a double-decker *(bed)*. I like making things flat *(iron)*. I like to be in fashion *(shoes or clothes)*. Sometimes I go dizzy going round and round *(washing machine, tumble dryer or food mixer)*. Don't give up! Hang on in there *(wardrobe)*. If you get this you are definitely getting hotter *(fire or cooker)*. You could say I'm a water 'otter *(kettle, pan or coffee maker)*. I'm just so cool *(fridge or freezer)*. I got a face and hands *(clock)*.

Alternatively, or as well as, you could play this game . . .

Moving house
This is based on the game 'I went to the shop and I bought . . .' where children complete the initial phrase by adding an item. Then they take it in turns to add an item to the shopping list while repeating the whole list up to that point.

You could say: 'Into the furniture van went . . .' as your initial phrase and the idea of the game would be for the children to take turns adding to the list of objects to be found in the home. For example the first child might say: 'Into the furniture van went a *bed*.'

The next child would have to repeat that and add another item. And so on until the list cannot be remembered any longer. At which point another game can be started. (Why not keep a note of the longest list?)

Talky bit   Talk to the children about moving house. Ask if any of them have ever moved house. What was it like? How did they feel? Were they excited or sad to leave? Did they have to change school? And so on. Explain that today they are going to hear about someone who was told by God to leave his home and go and live in a place that he had never been to before.

Here's the background that you want to get across:
  • Abram was brought up in Ur in Babylonia, which is today called Iraq.
  • One day his father, Terah, decided to take all his family and leave Ur and go to Canaan, which is today called Israel and Palestine. However, he then decided to settle in Haran, which was one of the towns on the way.
  • Abram was married to Sarai but they had no children.

Pick up the story by reading about God's promise to Abram in Genesis 12:1-9 and then ask the following questions:

Was going to another land going to be an adventure? Was it going to be easy? If not, why not? Encourage the children to identify a little with Abram and Sarai. Comment on the fact that they would have to leave people they loved, they would have to leave their home and live in tents for a very long time as they made the journey to Canaan. What would this mean for them?

Write out the following verses (Genesis 12:2-3 – taken from the International Children's Bible) onto card or into PowerPoint to display so the children can read them together (don't include the actions). Then ask the children to read with you God's promise to Abram and join in the actions.

I will make you a great nation (*thumbs up and indicate a large crowd*)
And I will bless you (*mime 'giving' with both hands*)
I will make you famous (*look amazed, open and close hands while saying 'Wow'*)
I will bless those who bless you (*mime 'giving' with both hands*)
I will curse those who curse you (*turn head away while miming a shunning action with both hands*)
And all the people of the earth (*mime world shape*)
Will be blessed through you (*mime 'giving' with both hands*)

Summarise by saying that God had promised Abram and Sarai that if they left their country and went to the land he was going to show them then he would bless them, help them and start a whole new family through them. Abram and Sarai were obedient to God and obeyed his command to go to Canaan.

God might not ask us to go to another country to live (although he might!) but he does want us to obey him. There are many of God's commands in the Bible and if we obey them then he promises to look after us and bless us.

If he should ask us to do something specific for him then he wants us to be like Abram. He wants us to obey because it will mean blessing for us and others as well.

ACTIVITY 46

Obstacle course – trust me!

Trust in the Lord with all your heart. Never rely on what you know.
Proverbs 3:5 (Good News Bible)

You will need
- An obstacle course
- Some blindfolds
- More helpers than usual, if you have a large group (use your own judgement)

How it works   Set up an obstacle course, such as a table to go under, a bowl of water to avoid, a bowl of cereal to eat a spoonful from, a tight rope to step over (not too high), or any other ingenious ideas you might have.

Line the children up in twos, one blindfolded, the other calling out instructions that will lead them safely through the obstacle course (no contact allowed!)

The instructions will be words such as left, right, forward, stop, head down, lift right leg and so on. If you have a large group you might want to set up more than one obstacle course, because undoubtedly everyone will want a go. This is why you will need more helpers than usual.

Talky bit   If you used Activity 45 recap the story so far and explain that Abram and Sarai were now in Canaan and nearly 25 years had gone by. Abram was now 99 years old and God told him again that he was going to have a son. God also changed his name from Abram which meant exalted father (an important man) to Abraham, which meant father of many. Sarai's name was also changed to Sarah and although both names meant princess, her new name also implied that she was going to be a mother.

Important event 1: Read the story of the three visitors (Genesis 18:1-16). And then ask one of the children to read Genesis 21:1-17.
Important event 2: Read the story of God testing Abraham in Genesis 22:1-18.

Draw out the point that Abraham trusted God and this made it much easier to obey him. He knew that God had promised that there was going to be a whole new nation born from him and Sarah. Do you think Abraham knew God was testing him? We don't know for sure, but we do know that he was wiling to take the chance that God would accept his son as an offering. (The only person God accepted as a human offering was Jesus. Jesus agreed to die for us so that we could be forgiven, let off all the wrong things we've ever done, and be God's friend.)

Close by saying that God wants us to learn to trust him and obey him. We can believe that he always wants what's best for us, and that he will always be there for us.

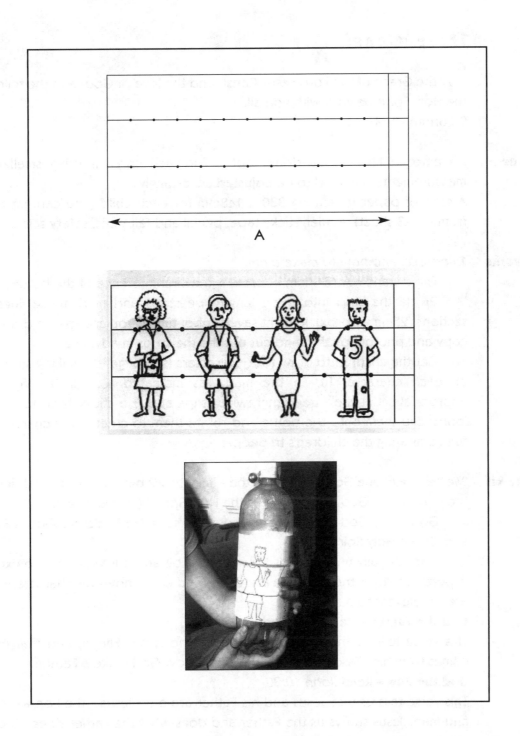

ACTIVITY 47

Three in one!

May the Grace of the Lord Jesus Christ, and the love of God, and the fellowship of the Holy Spirit be with with you all.
2 Corinthians 13:14

You will need   An empty 2-litre plastic drinks bottle for each child. If using smaller bottles, measurements will need to be adjusted accordingly.
A strip of paper measuring 330 x 148mm for each child (you can get two strips from an A3 sheet), a ruler, sticky tape, pencil and felt pens, safety scissors.

How it works   *Tri-people, and how to make them:*
The distance 'A' (311mm approx) is the circumference of the bottle.

Divide the strip into three lengthwise strips and mark these lines into 12 sections (25mm approx). It might save a lot of time if you are able to draw a master copy and photocopy this, and cut out the the strips in advance.

Get the children to draw four characters (see page 91) making sure the body on each character fits in the marks as indicated. Colour the figures in as appropriate. Cut the three lengthwise strips and use sticky tape to make three loops. Slip them onto the bottle and rotate them to create new characters. Have fun comparing the children's tri-people.

Talky bit   'We believe in one God, the Father, the Almighty. We believe in one Lord, Jesus Christ, the only Son of God. We believe in the Holy Spirit.' (Nicene Creed)

God is one God – but three individual persons. God is Father, God is Son (Jesus) and God is Holy Spirit.

Nobody fully understands how this can be and it is very hard to explain. The important thing is that all three are God – and each shows his characteristics. They are all relevant to our daily life.

God the Father – Read *1 Corinthians 8:6a*
This verse tells us that there is one God who is our Father, and that everything comes from him. Talk to the children about how God is like a Father.

God the Son – Read *John 10:30*
This verse tells us that Jesus and his Father are one. Jesus – the Son – is both God and man. Jesus shows us the Father and does what the Father does. God sent his Son to earth as a human to die for our sins so that we could be forgiven.

God the Holy Spirit – Read *John 14:16*
Jesus says that he will ask his Father to send the Holy Spirit who would be a helper, comforter and teacher. The Holy Spirit is God and with us today.

ACTIVITY 48

If you want to tell people about the flavour, you have to eat the cake!

But you will receive power when the Holy Spirit comes on you; and you will be my witnesses in Jerusalem, and in all Judea and Samaria, and to the ends of the earth. Acts 1:8

You will need A wonderfully tasty cake, some paper plates, and handwipes.

How it works Buy a cake, or even better, get the best cake baker in church to bake you a very special cake.

Begin by giving a piece to everyone in the group except one (save them a piece for later). This person could be a leader or an older child whom you have previously briefed, and who would be good at improvisation.

As the group is eating, make it clear to everyone that your stooge hasn't had any, for example by whizzing the plate past them so that they don't have time to take a piece. When everyone has finished, explain that you thought it would be nice to have this lovely cake in your time together today. Ask the stooge what they thought of the cake.

The answer should be vaguely truthful but with a number of clearly false statements included. For example: 'Well, I thought it looked absolutely delicious, all that chocolate icing on the top and cherries. I love cherries. It was such a surprise when I tasted it, though: I never expected to find all those currants inside.'

Pretty soon the children should start reacting because they know that the stooge is wrong: it wasn't a chocolate cake, there were no cherries, it didn't contain currants (or whatever is appropriate for your particular cake).

How do they know the stooge is wrong? Because they have eaten it and the stooge hasn't. You could get a child to give a more accurate description of the cake for the other person's benefit before presenting them with their own piece to try.

Make the point that the ones who had experienced the cake for themselves were the ones who were best qualified to talk on the subject.

Talky bit After Jesus had risen from the dead on Easter Sunday he spent the next 40 days here on earth being seen many times and by lots of people, including the disciples.

On one occasion 500 people all saw him at once. The disciples were really glad to have Jesus with them again. They probably would have been glad to go on like this for ever, but Jesus had told them that he wouldn't always be with them in his earthly body: he had to go back to his Father in heaven. But Jesus promised that when he had gone he would ask his Father to send the Holy Spirit to stay with the disciples for ever.

Read Acts 2:1-11 to describe the full wonder of the coming of the Holy Spirit.

ACTIVITY 49

Experiments session

Be good servants and use your gifts to serve each other.
1 Peter 4:10b

You will need
- A jug marked 'A'
- A second jug marked 'B' containing white vinegar
- A jar of white powder – bicarbonate of soda
- Two empty jam jars or similar

(NB *You will need one set of these items if you do it as a presentation from the front, or a set for each group, complete with instructions (and extra supervisors) if you all have a go.*)

How it works
You could do this as a presentation at the front, but it's preferable to give the children the equipment and the instructions to do it in small groups and to try to make the connection (you'll see) for themselves.

Put a dessertspoonful of powder into the first jam jar.
Add some liquid (water) from jug 'A'.
Note carefully what, if anything, happens.

Put a spoonful of the powder into the second jam jar.
Add some liquid from jug 'B'.
Note carefully what, if anything, happens.

Read 1 Peter 4:10-11.

Talky bit
What have the experiments you've just done got to do with these verses?

The white powder in this glass is representative of us as Christians. We all know that we have work to do for God. For example, we know that we should witness to our friends about Jesus. Sometimes we can get on with doing God's work in our own strength and then it can seem like really hard work with little result. What happened to the white powder when we added the liquid from jug 'A'? Nothing: it just got wet!

But instead of going ahead in our own strength we can ask God to fill us with the Holy Spirit so that we can work in his strength. Then the difference can be quite spectacular! The Holy Spirit has been called 'The Giving Gift'. When the Father gives us the Holy Spirit, he in turn gives gifts to us.

We're going to look at those in our next session.

ACTIVITY 50

Potted sports event

[The people] were filled with wonder and amazement at what had happened to him.
Acts 3:10

You will need
- Cones, tape measure, stop watch, bean bags, balls and a wheelchair
- Some extra helpers to act as marshals

How it works
Have a mini-Olympics or potted sports event, including various activities such as standing long jump; standing high jump; hopping to a cone and back as many times as possible in a short space of time (add simple 'sports' events to make it a fun occasion). You could include a simple wheelchair obstacle course to celebrate the Paralympics, in keeping with the first element of the Talky bit.

Talky bit
1 Corinthians 12 mentions nine different gifts that the Holy Spirit gives to the Church. We are going to look briefly at two incidents in the life of the early Church where we can see some of the gifts being used.

1. **Healing and faith** Acts 3:1-12
    Peter and John meet the man by the Beautiful Gate in Jerusalem. The man has been crippled from birth so he asks passers-by, including Peter and John, for money. They tell him that they haven't any money but by the power of Jesus they can make him walk. Peter takes him by the hand and helps him to his feet. The man starts leaping and jumping around and praising God. People had seen him sitting begging day after day and now here he was walking and jumping! They wanted to know what had happened so Peter told them all about Jesus and what God had done through him. Two thousand more people were saved that day.

2. **Miracles** Acts 16:23-34
    Paul and Silas had gone to the town of Philippi to tell the people there about Jesus but they upset some of the people there and now they are in jail. The jailer has been ordered to guard them carefully so he puts them far inside the jail and fastens their feet between large blocks of wood. About midnight Paul and Silas are praying and praising God, and the other prisoners are listening. Suddenly there is a big earthquake that shakes the foundations of the jail. The doors of the prison break open and all the prisoners are freed from their chains.

    The jailor wakes up, and seeing the prison doors open he assumes that all the prisoners have escaped. He takes his sword and is about to kill himself when Paul shouts to him: 'Don't hurt yourself! We are all here!' The jailor, on discovering that this is perfectly true, falls down before Paul and Silas and asks them: 'What must I do to be saved?' Paul and Silas tell him to believe in the Lord Jesus, and the jailor